Cross Stitch GIFTS *for Special Occasions*

NICHOLAS
1
2
3
4
5
6
7
8
9
10
11
12
13
14
15
16
17
18
19
20
21
22
23
24

JULIE HASLER

Cross Stitch GIFTS for Special Occasions

CASSELL

First published in the UK 1996
by Cassell Publishers Ltd
Wellington House
125 Strand
LONDON
WC2R 0BB

Designed by Maggie Aldred

Photographed by Paul Bricknell

Distributed in the United States
by Sterling Publishing Co., Inc.
387 Park Avenue South, New York, NY 10016–8810

A British Library Cataloguing in Publication Data block for this book may be obtained from the British Library

ISBN 0–304–34437–0
Typeset by Keystroke, Jacaranda Lodge, Wolverhampton
Printed and bound in Spain by Graficromo S.A., Cordoba

Contents

INTRODUCTION

In recent years, the popularity of creating beautiful craft work by hand has been increasing among women and men of all age groups. More and more people are turning to the gentle and relaxing craft of cross stitch to add a personal touch to a never-ending variety of items, from small greetings cards and gifts right up to larger items for home furnishings.

Cross stitch is a very rewarding and inexpensive hobby. It is also very easy to learn. There are only a few simple basic rules, and once you have mastered these, you can attempt any design. With a little practice, you will be able to achieve results that even an experienced stitcher would be proud of. Whether you are an experienced needleworker or a complete beginner, you will find projects in this book to suit your abilities. The wealth of designs covers a wide range of special occasions and incorporates gift ideas for friends and all members of the family – including projects and designs for men.

If you are a busy stitcher, with little spare time on your hands, you will really appreciate the small-scale designs in this book. Most of the greetings cards and gifts are simple to create, using the minimum of materials, and you can be sure that the effort you put into them will be much appreciated by the recipients.

If you have more time available create your own, larger projects by combining motifs from different charts, and experimenting with the alphabets and numerals. You could even use different colourways, to make designs that are uniquely yours.

Happy stitching!

Bride Groom

MATERIALS AND TECHNIQUES

MATERIALS

A few basic sewing materials – fabrics, needles and threads, an embroidery hoop and, of course, scissors – are all that are required in order to work the cross stitch designs in this book.

Fabrics

Fabrics used for cross stitch have an even weave: that is, the number of vertical threads matches the number of horizontal threads exactly, making them easy to count. Aida, Hardanger and Linda are examples of evenweave fabrics that are available in a wide choice of colours, including white, ecru, black, red, blue, green and yellow. They also come with varying numbers of threads, or blocks of threads, to 2.5cm (1in). This is known as the thread 'count' of the fabric, and it will determine the size of the cross stitches and thus of each of the finished designs.

The type of fabric to be used is specified with each project. Do not use a fabric which does not have an even weave, as this will distort the embroidery either horizontally or vertically.

Needles

Cross stitch is worked with small, blunt tapestry needles. These are available in numbered sizes: size 24 is suitable for fabrics up to 14 threads to 2.5cm (1in) and 26 for finer work.

Threads

The designs in this book have been created using DMC six-stranded embroidery cottons. The number

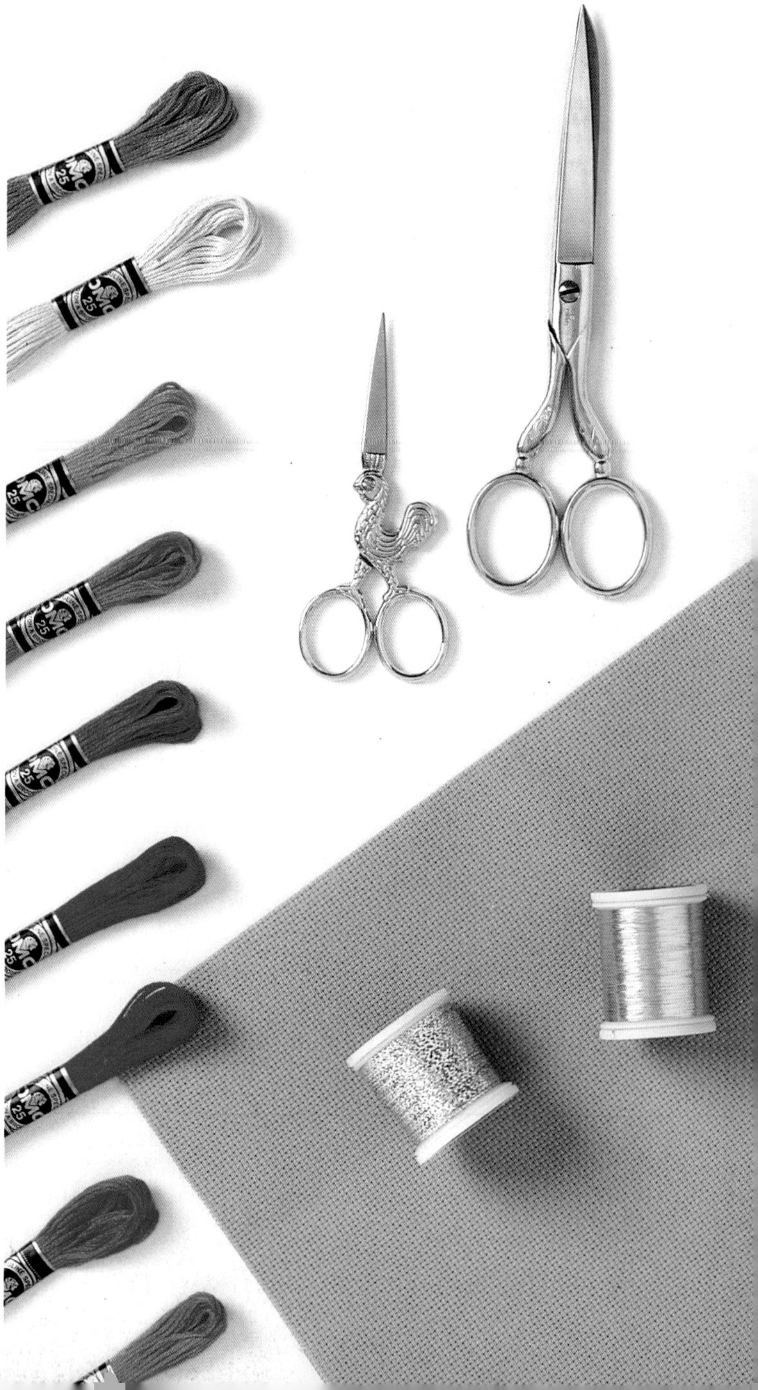

DMC 25

of strands you use will depend upon the fabric you decide to work on. Details are given with each project, but generally three strands are used for fabrics with 11 threads per 2.5cm (1in), two strands for those with 14, 16 and 18 threads to 2.5cm (1in), and one strand for finer work. DMC non-divisible metallic threads and Kreinik blending filament have also been incorporated into a number of the design projects.

Embroidery hoops

A circular embroidery hoop with screw-type tension adjuster is ideal for holding your fabric flat and taut as you stitch. Hoops are available in plastic or wood, and in several sizes: choose from diameters of 10, 12.5 or 15cm (4, 5 or 6in), according to the size of the design you are stitching.

Scissors

You will need two pairs of scissors. A pair of sharp embroidery scissors is essential for snipping threads close to the work, and especially if a mistake has to be unpicked. You will also need a pair of dressmaking scissors for cutting fabrics.

PREPARING TO STITCH

To prevent the cut edges of the fabric unravelling, you can either cover them with a fold of masking tape, or use whip stitching or machine stitching to secure.

Following a chart

In this book, each square on a chart represents one cross stitch to be worked on the fabric. The symbol in the square denotes the thread colour to be used, and corresponds to the colour key listed with each chart. This gives a colour description for each symbol, plus the DMC shade number. The letters BF indicate Kreinik blending filament, and follow the relevant shade number. HL denotes high-lustre filament.

Backstitch is shown on a chart as a solid line, the length of one square representing a single stitch. Again, the thread colour and DMC or Kreinik blending filament shade number are given in the colour key provided with each chart.

Positioning the design

Where you make your first stitch is important, as this will determine the position of the finished design on your fabric. First, you will need to find the exact centre point of the chart, by following the arrows on the chart to their intersection. Next, locate the centre of your fabric by folding it in half vertically and then horizontally, pinching along the folds. Mark along these lines with tacking stitches if you prefer. The centre stitch of your design will lie where the folds in the fabric meet.

It is best to begin stitching at the top of the design. To locate the top, count the squares up from the centre of the chart, and then count left or right to the first symbol. Next, count the corresponding number of holes up and across from the centre of the fabric and begin at that point. Remember that each square on the chart represents one stitch on the fabric.

Mounting the fabric in a hoop

To mount the fabric in an embroidery hoop, place the area to be embroidered over the inner ring and carefully push the outer ring over it. Pull the fabric gently and evenly, ensuring that it is drum taut in the hoop and that the mesh is straight, and tightening the screw adjuster as you go. When stitching, you will find that it easier to have the screw in the 'ten o'clock' position to prevent your thread from becoming tangled in it with each stitch. (If you are left handed, you should have the screw in the 'one o'clock' position.)

As you work, you will find that you have to retighten the fabric from time to time to keep it taut. This tension makes stitching easier, allowing the needle to be pushed through the holes without piercing the fibres of the fabric.

Using stranded cottons

When working with stranded cotton, always separate the strands and place them together again before threading your needle and beginning to stitch. Never double the thread: for example, if you need to use two strands, use two separate strands placed together, not one doubled up. These simple steps allow for much better coverage of the fabric, giving a neater finish.

Using blending filament

Blending filament is used in conjunction with other threads. The different fibres have different degrees of elasticity, and control is essential, so follow the instructions below to knot the blending filament on the needle first, and then add the other thread.

1 Loop the filament and pass the loop through the eye of the needle, leaving a short tail (Fig 1).
2 Pass the loop over the end of the needle (Fig 2).
3 Tighten the loop at the end of the eye (Fig 3).
4 Gently stroke the knotted filament once to 'lock' it in place.

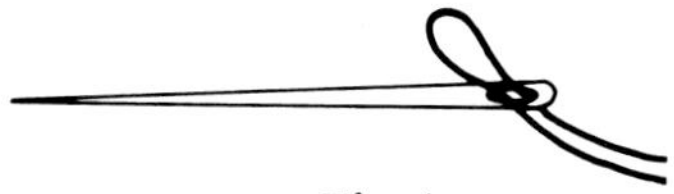

Fig 1

Fig 2

Fig 3

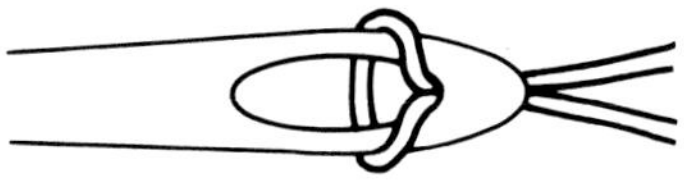

Fig 4

Using metallic threads

Several different metallic threads have been used in the designs in this book. These are used singly, straight from the reel.

STITCH TECHNIQUES

The designs in this book are worked in counted cross stitch. In some of the designs, backstitch has been used for numbers and lettering, and to provide further detail and outlining.

Cross stitch

To start a new thread, bring the needle up through a hole from the wrong side of the fabric. Fasten the thread by holding a short length on the underside of the fabric and securing it with the first three or four stitches you make (Fig 5). Never use knots to fasten your thread, as this will create a bumpy back surface and prevent your work from lying flat when completed.

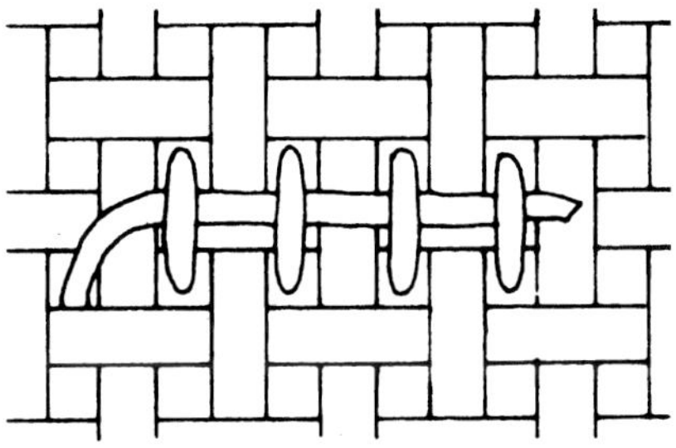

Fig 5

To begin the stitch, bring the needle across one thread (or block of threads) to the right and one square above on the diagonal, and insert the needle (Fig 6). Half the stitch is now complete. Continue in this way until the end of the row of stitches in that colour is reached. Your stitches should be diagonal on the right side of the fabric and vertical on the

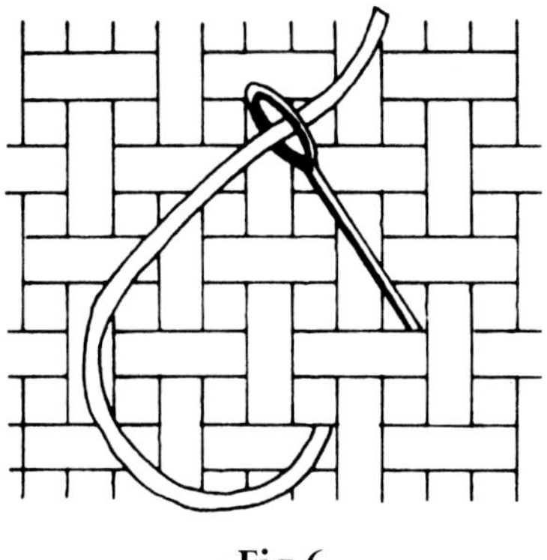

Fig 6

wrong side. Complete the upper half of the stitches by crossing back in the opposite direction to form a cross (Figs 7 and 8). Work vertical rows of stitches as shown in Fig 9.

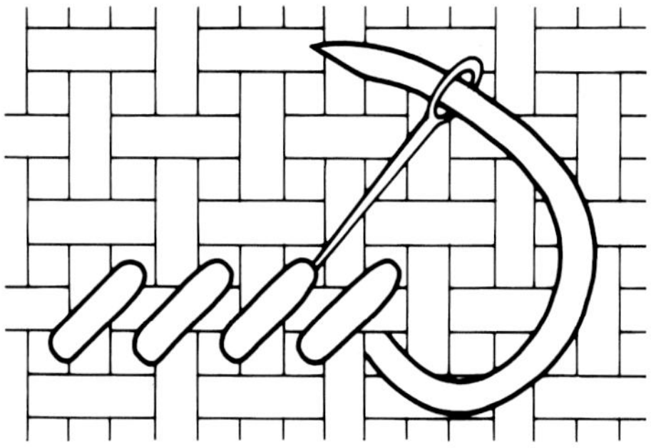

Fig 7

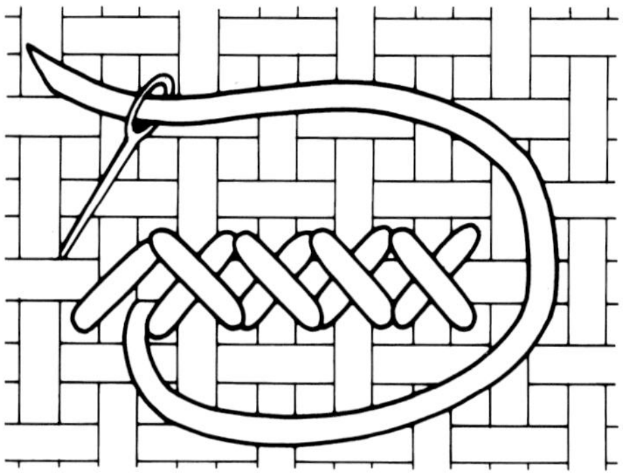

Fig 8

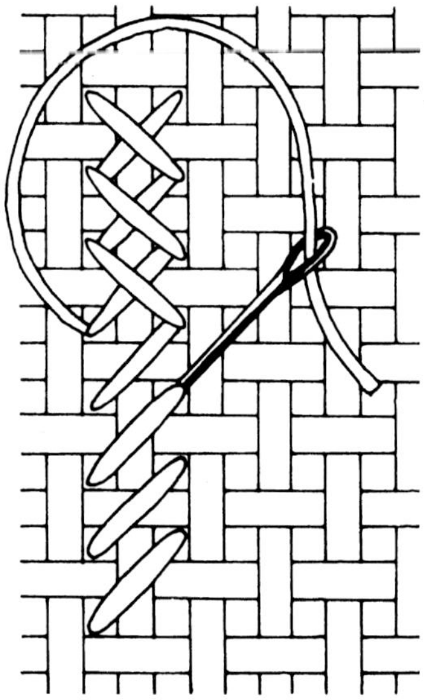

Fig 9

Cross stitch can also be worked by crossing each stitch as you come to it, as you would do for isolated stitches. This methods works just as well – it is really a matter of personal preference. Whichever method is used, it is important that all the top stitches face in the same direction, otherwise the finished embroidery will look uneven and messy.

Finish all threads by running your needle under four or more stitches on the wrong side of the work (Fig 10) and snip off the thread neatly.

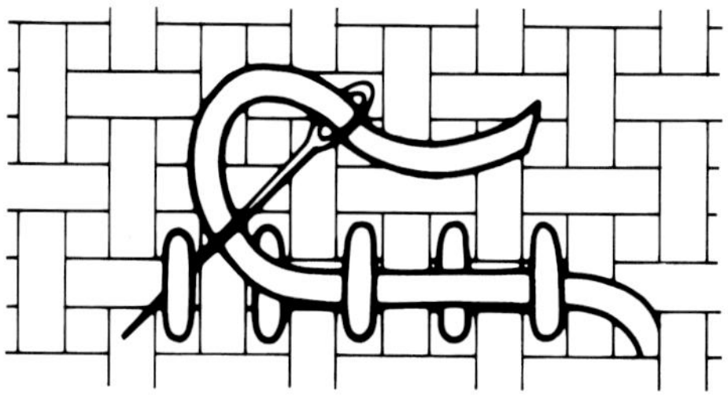

Fig 10

Backstitch

Backstitch is used in some of the designs in the book, mainly for outlines and finer details. Work any backstitch when your cross stitch embroidery has been completed. Always use one strand less than you used for the embroidery; for example, if three strands of stranded cotton have been used to work the cross stitch, use two strands for the backstitching. If only one strand of stranded cotton has been used to work the cross stitch, use one strand also for the backstitching.

Backstitch is worked from hole to hole and can be stitched in diagonal, vertical or horizontal lines, as shown in Fig 11. Bring the needle up from the wrong side of the fabric at 1 and take it back down again at 2. Bring it up again at 3, down at 4, up at 5 and so on, following the direction indicated by the line on the chart. Always take care not to pull the stitches too tight, otherwise the contrast of colour will be lost against the cross stitches. Finish off the threads in the same way as for cross stitch.

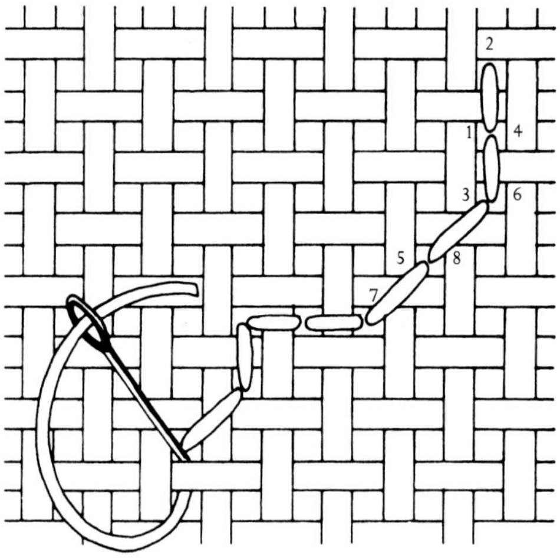

Fig 11

Useful tips

- It is important not to pull the fabric out of shape when you are stitching. Work the stitches in two motions – straight up through a hole in the fabric and then straight down, ensuring that the fabric remains taut. Make sure that you pull the thread snug, but *not* tight. If you use this method, the thread will lie just where you want it to and will not pull your fabric out of shape.
- If your thread becomes twisted while working, drop your needle and let it hang down freely. It will then untwist itself. Do not continue working with twisted thread, as it will appear thinner and will not cover your fabric so well.
- Never leave your needle in the design area of your work when not in use. No matter how good the needle might be, it could rust in time and may mark your work permanently.
- Do not carry thread across an open expanse of fabric. If you are working separate areas of the same colour, finish off and begin again. Loose threads, especially in dark colours, will be visible from the right side of your work when the project is completed.

Pressing

When you have completed your cross stitch embroidery, it may need to be pressed. To protect your work, place the embroidery right side down on a soft towel and cover the reverse side with a thin, slightly damp cloth before pressing.

AFTERCARE

You may find that at some stage your cross stitch projects will need to be laundered. This is no problem: just follow the simple advice below which is specially recommended by DMC for items stitched with their stranded embroidery cottons.

The following recommendations are for washing embroidery separate from all other laundry.

COTTON OR LINEN	SYNTHETICS
Recommended washing	
Wash in warm, soapy water. Rinse thoroughly. Squeeze without twisting and hang to dry.	Not recommended.
Bleaching or whitening agent	
Dilute the product according to the manufacturer's instructions. Pre-soak the embroidery in clear water first, then soak for five minutes in a solution of about one tablespoon of the product per litre (2 pints) of cold water. Rinse thoroughly in cold water.	These instructions are recommended if the white of the fabric is not of a high standard. If the fabric is a pure white (white with a bluish tinge), do not use bleaching or whitening agent.
Dry cleaning	
Avoid dry cleaning. Some spot removers (benzine, trichloroethylene) can be used on small occasional stains.	Not recommended, even for small stains.

MAKING UP THE PROJECTS

The cross stitch embroidery in this book can be made up into a wide range of pictures, greetings cards and gift items. If you are stitching designs for a number of cards or small items, you can economize on fabric by cutting a piece large enough for several designs (remembering to space them well), rather than cutting a small piece for each design. Full instructions for making up pictures, cards, trinket boxes, gift bags and more are given in this chapter; for individual one-off projects, making-up instructions are provided alongside the stitching method and chart for each design.

MOUNTING AND FRAMING

When you have completed your cross stitch embroidery, you may wish to mount it in preparation for framing as a picture. A number of the designs in this book have been made up in this way, using frames in a variety of sizes and styles. Make sure you choose acid-free board on which to mount your embroidery, otherwise unsightly brown patches may appear after a while.

YOU WILL NEED

Completed cross stitch embroidery, worked centrally on fabric 2.5–4cm (1–1½in) larger all round than your chosen mounting board
Mounting board
Pins
Masking tape

1 Press your completed cross stitch embroidery. Place the embroidered fabric face down on a clean, flat surface and position the mounting board centrally on top of it.

2 Fold one edge of the fabric over the mounting board, ensuring that it is perfectly straight, and secure it with pins along the edge of the board. Secure the opposite edge in the same way, making sure that the fabric is straight and taut on the board.

3 Use masking tape to secure the edges of the fabric on the back of the mounting board and then remove the pins.

4 Repeat steps 2 and 3 with the remaining two edges.

If this procedure seems a little too fiddly to attempt, there is now a wonderful range of self-stick mounting boards available in five different sizes from most large department stores and good craft shops. These really are a treat to work with, and make the job very easy:

You simply cut the board to size as before, peel off the backing, lay your needlework fabric centrally on the board and, when you are completely satisfied with the positioning, press down very hard over the entire needlework surface. Tape the excess fabric carefully to the back of the mounting board with masking tape.

Your embroidery picture is now ready to be framed. The best results will be achieved if you take

it to a professional framer. If you are having glass in your frame, the effect will be improved by using the non-reflective type. Although slightly more expensive, it is well worth it.

FLEXI-HOOPS

Flexi-hoops are manufactured in a range of different colours and sizes, and in oval, landscape and circular shapes. They offer a superb method of finishing off a cross stitch project, giving a professional touch at a very reasonable price.

YOU WILL NEED

Completed cross stitch embroidery, worked centrally on fabric 5cm (2in) larger all round than your chosen flexi-hoop
DMC flexi-hoop

1 Press your completed cross stitch embroidery.
2 To mount it in the flexi-hoop, place the embroidered area centrally over the inner ring and gently push the flexible outer ring over it, ensuring that the fabric is drum taut in the hoop and that the mesh is straight.
3 Turn to the wrong side, and trim off the excess fabric using a pair of sharp dressmaking scissors.

GREETINGS CARDS

Personalized greetings cards containing a small embroidery are a pleasure to make or to receive, and also a wonderful way of showing someone that you care. These cards will be treasured long after shop-bought ones have been forgotten. There are many types of card mounts on the market so you will have plenty of choice, but the basic method of assembly is the same.

YOU WILL NEED

Completed cross stitch embroidery, worked centrally on fabric slightly smaller than your chosen card mount
DMC or Framecraft greetings card mount
Ultra-soft, medium-weight iron-on bonding web (optional)
Double-sided adhesive tape

If you are stitching designs for a number of cards or small items, you can economize on fabric by cutting a piece large enough for several designs (remembering to space them well), rather than cutting a small piece for each design.
1 Press your completed embroidery and then iron the bonding web on to the wrong side of the fabric to prevent it from fraying.
2 Centralize the design in the card 'window'.
3 Use double-sided adhesive tape to fix the design into the card and press the card backing down firmly (Fig 1).

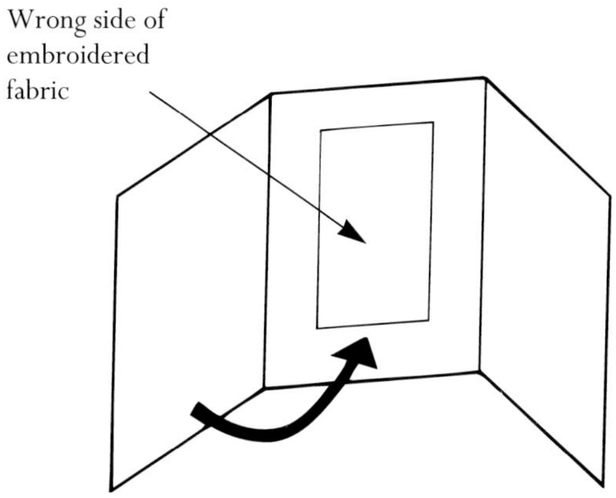

Fig 1

TRINKET BOWLS

Trinket bowls designed especially to take a cross stitch embroidery in the lid are available in a range of sizes, colours and styles. Choose from enamel, porcelain, wood, gilt, frosted or cut glass, silver plate and more, to tone or contrast with your embroidery and create a perfect small keepsake gift.

YOU WILL NEED

Completed cross stitch embroidery, worked centrally on fabric slightly larger than the lid of your chosen trinket bowl
Framecraft trinket bowl
Ultra-soft, medium-weight iron-on bonding web (optional)
Soft pencil
Rubber-based glue

1 Press your completed embroidery and then iron the bonding web on to the wrong side of the fabric to prevent it from fraying.

2 Place the embroidery face up on a firm, flat surface. Gently remove all parts from the trinket box or bowl lid.

3 Use the rim of the lid to centralize the design and then draw around the outer edge on to the fabric using a soft pencil. Remove the lid and cut the fabric to size.

4 To assemble the lid, replace the clear acetate and place your embroidery centrally into the lid, with the right side to the acetate. Place the sponge behind your design. Push the metal locking disc very firmly into place using thumb pressure, with the raised side of the disc facing the sponge. When the locking disc is tightly in position, use a little rubber-based glue to secure the flock lid-lining card to it.

This method is also used for mounting cross stitch embroidery in specially designed handbag mirrors, such as the second project for Mother's Day on page 34.

PAPERWEIGHTS

Paperweights make unusual gifts, which can be put to a practical use on a desk or used as ornaments around the home. Those specially designed for use with cross stitch embroideries are available in several different shapes, including circular, scalloped and oval.

YOU WILL NEED

Completed cross stitch embroidery, worked centrally on fabric slightly larger than your chosen paperweight
Framecraft paperweight
Ultra-soft, medium-weight iron-on bonding web

1 Press your completed embroidery and then iron the bonding web on to the wrong side of the fabric to prevent it from fraying.

2 Place the embroidery on a firm, flat surface and use the paper template provided with the paperweight to draw around your design, making sure it is central.

3 Cut the fabric to size and place it right side down into the recess in the base of the paperweight. Place the paper template on the reverse side of your embroidery. Peel the backing off the protective base and carefully stick it to the base of the paperweight, taking care that the embroidery and template do not move out of position.

GIFT BAGS

These easy-to-make bags are a wonderful way of presenting a gift. Use afterwards as lavender bags or pot-pourri sachets.

YOU WILL NEED

For a gift bag 14 × 10cm (5½ × 4in):
Completed cross stitch embroidery, worked on 29cm (11½in) scalloped-edge Aida band, 10cm (4in) 54 stitches wide, in your chosen colour
Sewing thread to match Aida band
0.5m (20in) ribbon, 3mm (⅛in) wide, in your chosen colour
Mill Hill glass pebble beads in various colours
Size 24 tapestry needle

The position for the embroidery is determined by folding the Aida band in half (short ends together) to find the centre, and then working the cross stitch design centrally, 2.5cm (1in) up from the fold line (Fig 2).

1 Press your completed cross stitch embroidery.

2 Fold the band in half as before, placing wrong sides together and aligning the edges, and pin in position.

3 Turn over 5mm (¼in) hem at the top of both sections and machine or hand stitch. Then machine or hand stitch the two sides together, just inside the scalloped edge (Fig 3). Turn the bag right side out.

4 Tie a knot in one end of the ribbon and thread the required number of glass beads on to it, using a large-eyed tapestry needle. Tie a knot in the remaining end of the ribbon.

5 When you have completed the bag, add an appropriate gift and tie a pretty bow with the ribbon.

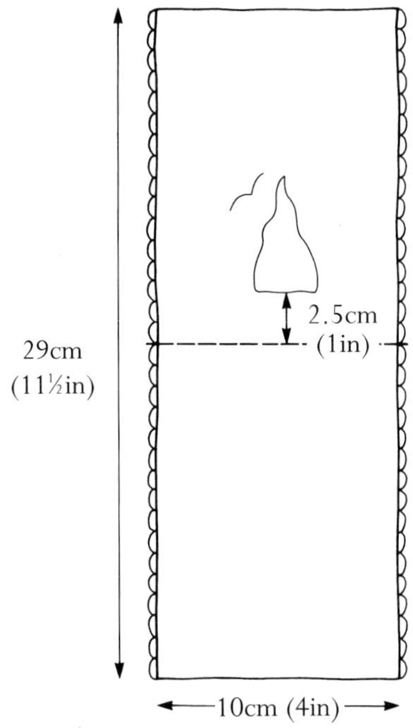

Fig 2

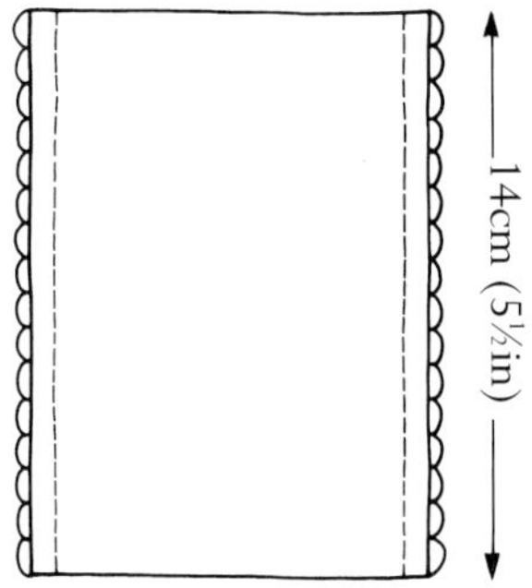

Fig 3

MINIATURE FRAMES

These delightful miniature frames make an attractive addition to any home. They are available in a range of materials and shapes, including circular, oval, rectangular and heart-shaped, and in a variety of colours.

YOU WILL NEED

Completed cross stitch embroidery, worked centrally on fabric slightly larger than your chosen frame
Framecraft miniature frame
Ultra-soft, medium-weight iron-on bonding web

1 Press your completed embroidery and iron the bonding web on to the wrong side of the fabric to prevent it from fraying.

2 Carefully dismantle all parts of the frame, and use the template provided to draw around your design, making sure that it is central. Cut the fabric to size.

3 To assemble the frame, replace the clear acetate and place your embroidery centrally into the frame with the right side towards the acetate, followed by the cardboard template and finally the backing. Secure the backing using the pins provided.

Valentine's Day

Hearts and flowers

The words 'I Love You' are encircled with a ring of hearts and flowers, ready for mounting in a small frame as a permanent memento of Valentine's Day. You could also mount the embroidery in a small hoop, or make it up into a charming gift bag.

Hearts and flowers

◪	**666**	Bright Christmas red
◫	**793**	Blue
☒	**743**	Dark yellow
—		**backstitch**
		666 Bright Christmas red

You will need

White Aida fabric to size,
14 threads/stitches to 2.5cm (1in)
10 × 7.5cm (4 × 3in) DMC rectangular
plastic frame
or
White Aida fabric to size,
18 threads/stitches to 2.5cm (1in)
7.5cm (3in) DMC flexi-hoop
or
Material as listed on page 17

For all:
Stranded cottons in the colours specified in the key

1 Work the cross stitch embroidery on the Aida fabric, using 2 strands of stranded cotton for the cross stitch and 1 strand for the backstitch. Position the design centrally on the fabric for the frame and flexi-hoop, and according to the instructions on page 17 for the gift bag.

2 Mount the embroidery in the frame or flexi-hoop following the instructions given on pages 17 and 15. Alternatively, make it up into a gift bag following the instructions given on page 17.

I
LOVE
YOU
I
LOVE
YOU
I
LOVE
YOU

LOVEHEART

This traditional heart-and-banner design can be displayed in an appropriately heart-shaped frame or mounted in a small flexi-hoop. It also looks pretty made up into a gift bag to give to a loved one.

YOU WILL NEED

White Aida fabric to size,
14 threads/stitches to 2.5cm (1in)
5.75cm (2¼in) DMC heart-shaped plastic frame
or
White Aida fabric to size,
18 threads/stitches to 2.5cm (1in)
7.5cm (3in) DMC flexi-hoop
or
Materials as listed on page 17

For all:
Stranded cottons in the colours specified in the key

1 Work the cross stitch embroidery on the Aida fabric, using 2 strands of stranded cotton for the cross stitch and 1 strand for the backstitch. Position the design centrally on the fabric for the frame and flexi-hoop, and according to the instructions on page 17 for the gift bag.

2 Mount the embroidery in the frame or flexi-hoop following the instructions given on pages 17 and 15. Alternatively, make it up into a gift bag following the instructions given on page 17.

LOVEHEART

◪	**666**	Bright Christmas red
⊡		White
—		**backstitch**
		413 Very dark steel grey

LOVE

I LOVE YOU

A pretty heart design for a trinket bowl, a gift bag or a paperweight.

YOU WILL NEED

White Aida fabric to size,
14 threads/stitches to 2.5cm (1in) 9cm (3½in)
Framecraft trinket bowl
or
White Aida fabric to size,
18 threads/stitches to 2.5cm (1in)
6.5cm (2½in) Framecraft scalloped paperweight
or
Materials listed on page 17

For all:
Stranded cottons in the colours specified in the key

1 Work the cross stitch embroidery on the Aida fabric, using 2 strands of stranded cotton for the cross stitch and 1 strand for the backstitch. Position the design centrally on the fabric for the frame and flexi-hoop, and according to the instructions on page 17 for the gift bag.
2 Mount the embroidery in the trinket bowl or paperweight following the instructions given on page 16. Alternatively, make it up into a gift bag following the instructions given on page 17.

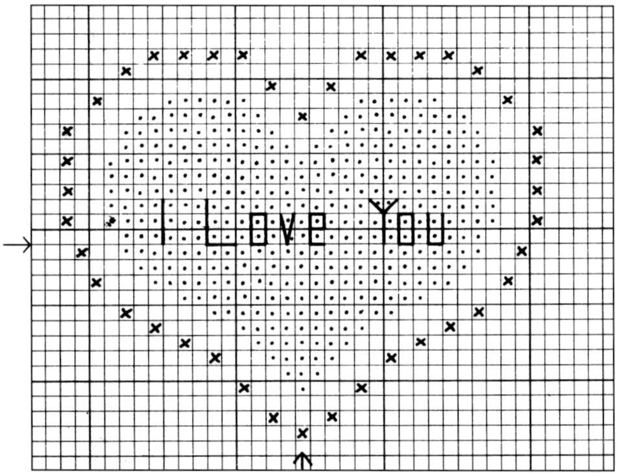

I LOVE YOU

•	**666**	Bright Christmas red
X	**3706**	Medium watermelon orange
—		**backstitch**
	413	Very dark steel grey

GOODNIGHT SWEETHEART

Make this romantic little 'pillow' for your sweetheart by following the design from the chart and personalizing it with letters from the alphabet on page 125.

YOU WILL NEED

19 × 18cm (7½ × 7in) white Aida fabric,
14 threads/stitches to 2.5cm (1in)
Matching sewing thread
19 × 18cm (7½ × 7in) contrasting fabric,
for backing
Stranded cottons in the colours specified in the key
1.1m (43in) white lace, 2.5cm (1in) deep
Small quantity of wadding

1 Work the cross stitch embroidery centrally on the Aida fabric, using 2 strands of stranded cotton for the cross stitch and 1 strand for the backstitch. Press the completed embroidery if required.
2 Cut out the heart shape by following the line

of the design, keeping 2.5cm (1in) outside the embroidery all the way round. Cut out the backing fabric to the same size.

3 Place the embroidered fabric face up on a firm, flat surface and pin the lace to the right side. Ensure that the sewing edge of the lace lies just over the stitching line (leave a 1.5cm (½in) seam allowance), with the frill to the centre. Tack carefully, so that the lace is gathered evenly all the way round. You may find it helpful to pin the lace to the fabric to keep it away from the seams.

4 With right sides together, pin the backing fabric to the embroidered Aida, and pin and tack in place. The lace is now sandwiched between the two fabrics. Either machine or hand stitch the fabrics together 1.5cm (½in) away from the edge of the embroidery, leaving a small opening for inserting the filling. Ensure that you do not catch the outside of the lace in the seam. Remove the tacking.

5 Turn the pillow right side out, releasing the lace frill, and fill evenly with wadding. Turn in the seam allowance and hand stitch the opening closed.

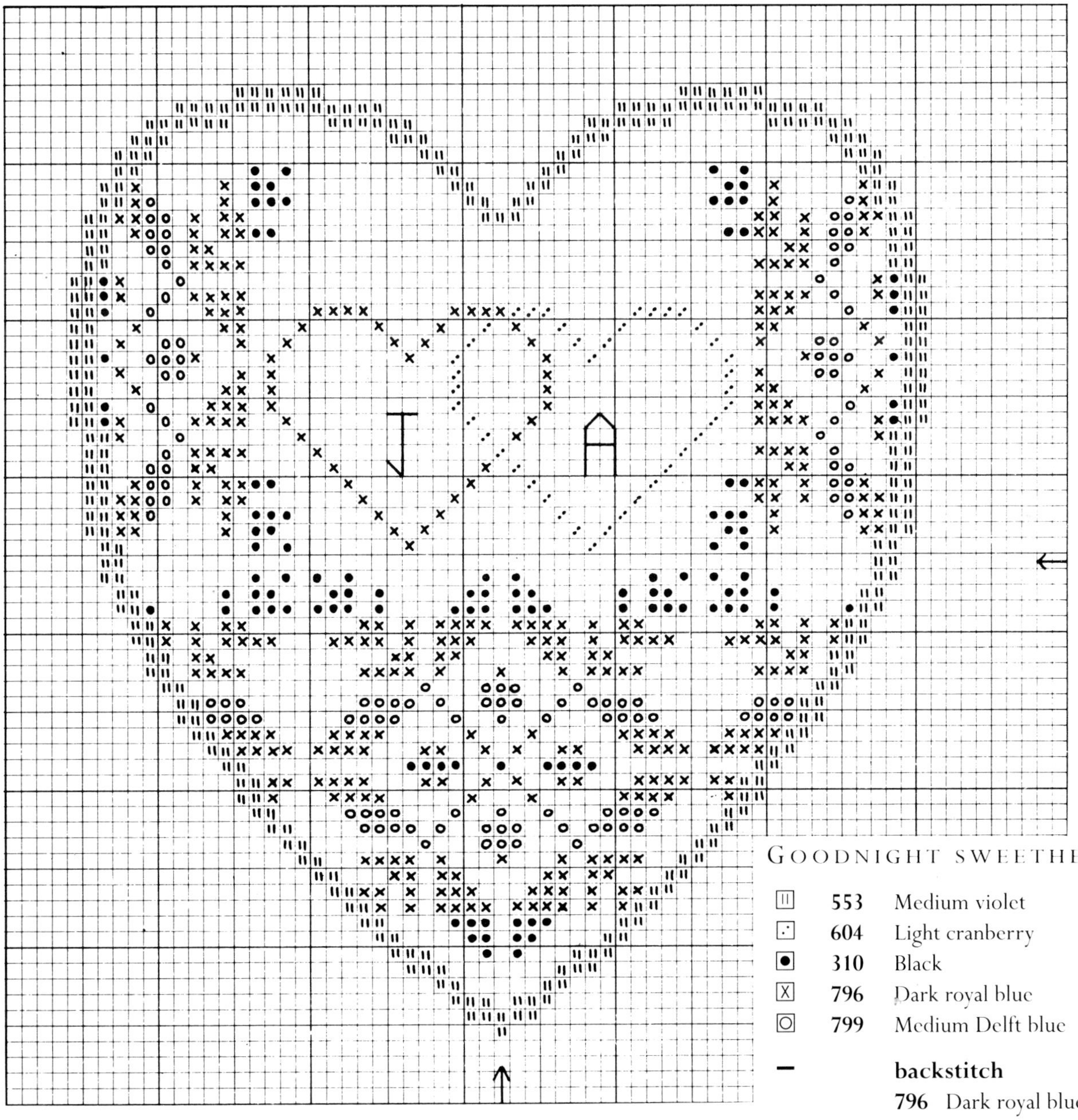

GOODNIGHT SWEETHEART

‖	**553**	Medium violet
⁛	**604**	Light cranberry
●	**310**	Black
X	**796**	Dark royal blue
O	**799**	Medium Delft blue
—		**backstitch**
		796 Dark royal blue

I love you
LOVE

SAY IT WITH HEARTS

A pastel bouquet of pink and yellow hearts, tied with a mauve bow, is beautifully displayed in this special keepsake card for Valentine's Day.

YOU WILL NEED

White Aida fabric to size,
14 threads/stitches to 2.5cm (1in)
Stranded cottons in the colours specified in the key
18 × 12cm (7¼ × 4¾in) DMC keepsake card

1 Work the cross stitch embroidery centrally on the Aida fabric, using 2 strands of stranded cotton throughout.
2 Mount the embroidery in the card following the instructions given on page 15.

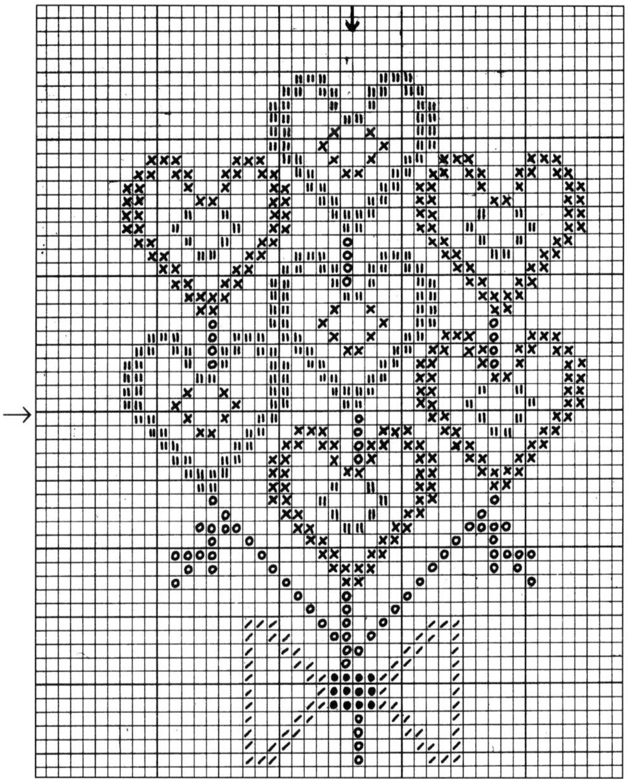

SAY IT WITH HEARTS

▥	**603**	Cranberry
☒	**726**	Light topaz yellow
◎	**912**	Light emerald green
◙	**550**	Very dark voilet
◪	**553**	Medium violet

LOVE IN THE AIR

A cascade of heart-shaped balloons surround the word 'Love' in this card design, which is worked in bright red and gold thread.

YOU WILL NEED

White Aida fabric to size,
14 threads/stitches to 2.5cm (1in)
Stranded cotton and metallic thread in
the colours specified in the key
18 × 12cm (7¼ × 4¾in) DMC keepsake card

1 Work the cross stitch embroidery centrally on the Aida fabric, using 2 strands of stranded cotton for the cross stitch and 1 strand for the backstitch, and the metallic thread straight from the reel.
2 Mount the embroidery in the card following the instructions given on page 15.

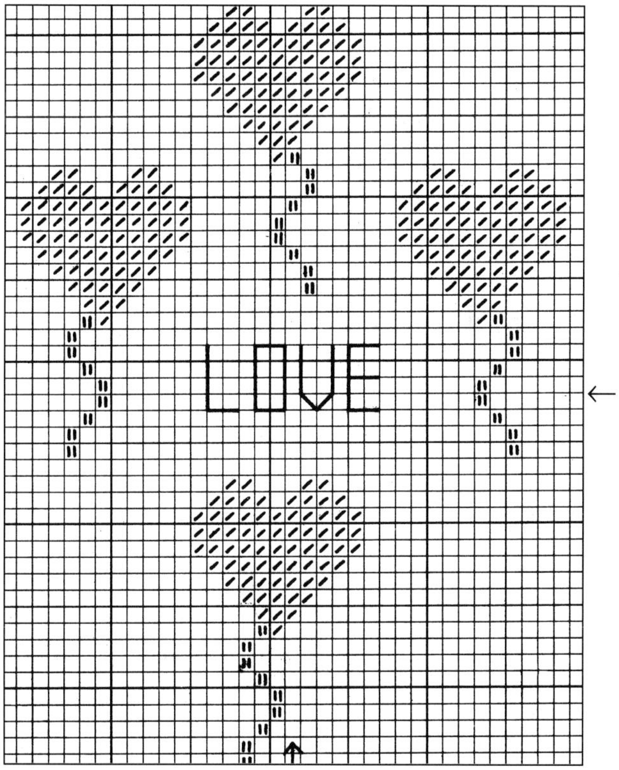

LOVE IN THE AIR

◪	**666**	Bright Christmas red
▥		Fil or clair gold thread
–		**backstitch**
		666 Bright Christmas red

*E*ASTER

EASTER PARADE

A traditional Easter bonnet and flowers, in a formal presentation card, reflect the springtime themes of the season.

YOU WILL NEED

White Hardanger fabric to size,
22 threads/stitches to 2.5cm (1in)
Stranded cottons in the colours specified in the key
9 × 11.5cm (3½ × 4½in) DMC presentation card

1 Work the cross stitch embroidery centrally on the Hardanger fabric, using 1 strand of stranded cotton throughout.
2 Mount the embroidery in the card following the instructions given on page 15.

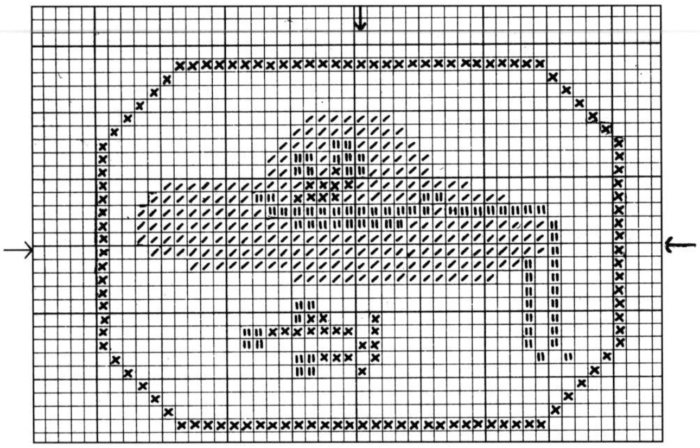

EASTER PARADE

‖	**335**	Dark pink
X	**703**	Chartreuse green
⁄	**437**	Light tan brown
·		White
P	**353**	Peach
●	**434**	Light brown
—		**backstitch**
		335 Dark pink

BUNNY WISHES

An Easter bunny wishes you 'Happy Easter' in this charming little greetings card, which is suitable for friends and relations of all ages.

YOU WILL NEED

White Hardanger fabric to size,
22 threads/stitches to 2.5cm (1in)
Stranded cottons in the colours specified in the key
7.5cm (3in) DMC studio card

1 Work the cross stitch embroidery centrally on the Hardanger fabric using 1 strand of stranded cotton throughout.
2 Mount the embroidery in the card following the instructions given on page 15.

BUNNY WISHES

‖	**335**	Dark pink
X	**703**	Chartreuse green
⁄	**437**	Light tan brown
·		White
P	**353**	Peach
●	**434**	Light brown
—		**backstitch**
		335 Dark pink

HAPPY EASTER

EASTER SQUARE

Easter eggs and flowers are surrounded by a pretty border and then framed in a dark-toned mount, to create a striking seasonal greetings card.

YOU WILL NEED

White Hardanger fabric to size,
22 threads/stitches to 2.5cm (1in)
Stranded cottons in the colours specified in the key
7.5cm (3in) square DMC studio card

1 Work the cross stitch embroidery centrally on the Hardanger fabric, using 1 strand of stranded cotton throughout.

2 Mount the embroidery in the card following the instructions given on page 15.

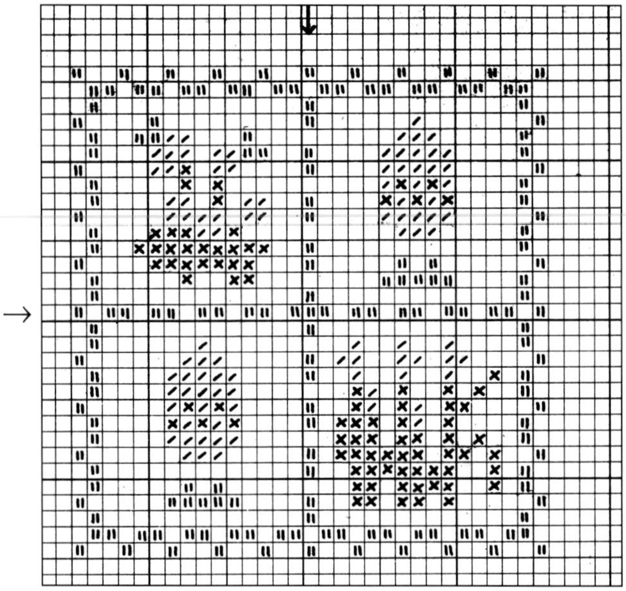

EASTER SQUARE

II	**335**	Dark pink
X	**703**	Chartreuse green
/	**437**	Light tan brown
·		White
P	**353**	Peach
●	**434**	Light brown
–		**backstitch**
		335 Dark pink

EASTER BUNNIES

A trio of Easter bunnies eagerly await their presents in this card which children will love to keep. The bunnies on their own can be mounted in a cool frosted-glass trinket bowl that will appeal to older children – and adults!

YOU WILL NEED

Cream Aida fabric to size,
14 threads/stitches to 2.5cm (1in)
10.5 × 17cm (4¼ × 6¾in) DMC keepsake card
or
Cream Aida fabric to size,
14 threads/stitches to 2.5cm (1in)
7cm (2⅝in) Framecraft frosted-glass trinket bowl

For both:
Stranded cottons in the colours specified in the key

1 Work the cross stitch embroidery centrally on the Aida fabric, using 2 strands of stranded cotton for the cross stitch and 1 strand for the backstitch.

2 Mount the embroidery in the card or trinket bowl following the instructions given on pages 15–16.

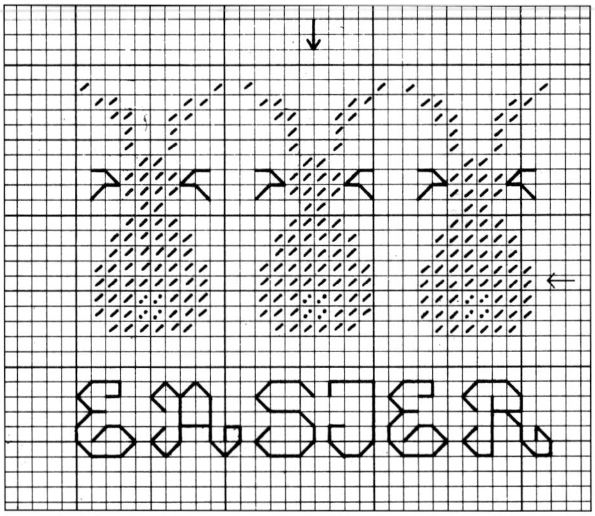

EASTER BUNNIES

/	**869**	Hazelnut brown
·		White
–		**backstitch**
		lettering **333** Dark lilac
		whiskers **318** Light steel grey

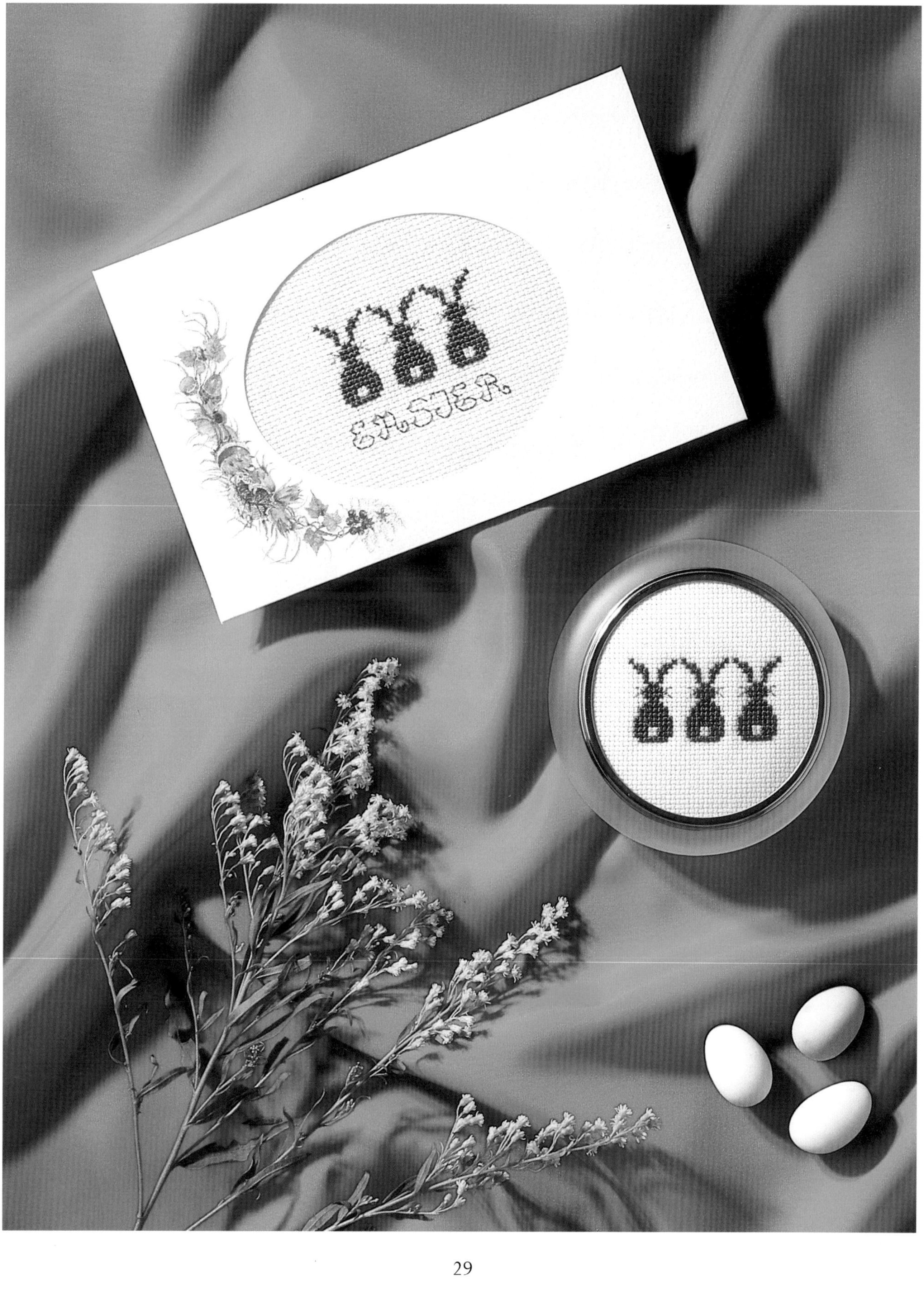
EASTER

EASTER SURPRISE

A gaily coloured Easter egg wrapped in a huge bow invites you to look inside a keepsake card decorated in complementary colours.

YOU WILL NEED

Cream Aida fabric to size,
14 threads/stitches to 2.5cm (1in)
Stranded cottons in the colours specified in the key
17 × 10.5cm (6¾in × 4¼in) DMC keepsake card

1 Work the cross stitch embroidery centrally on the Aida fabric, using 2 strands of stranded cotton for the cross stitch and 1 strand for the backstitch.

2 Mount the embroidery in the card following the instructions given on page 15.

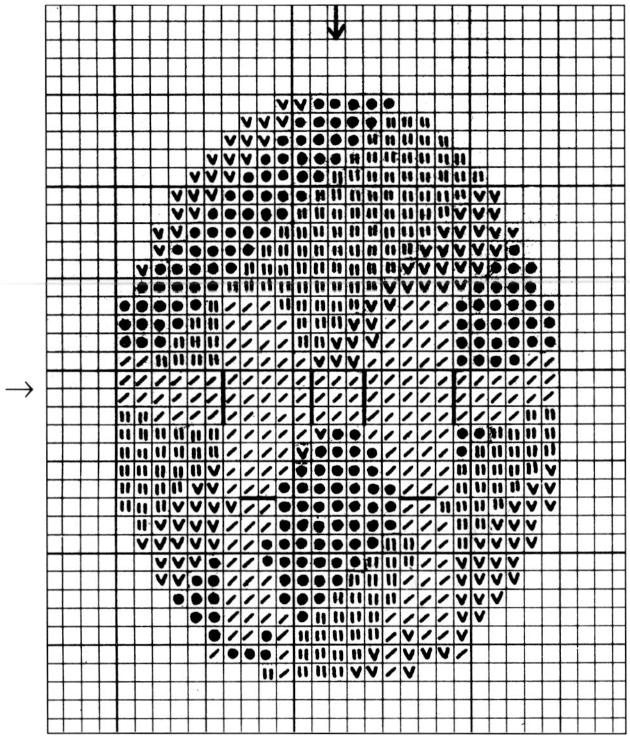

EASTER SURPRISE

⧄	743	Dark yellow
[V]	333	Dark lilac
[●]	809	Delft blue
[II]	911	Medium emerald green
—		**backstitch**
		977 Golden brown

EASTER CHICKS

Two lively chicks present the recipient of this card with an Easter basket. The chicks can also be used to decorate a trinket bowl.

YOU WILL NEED

Cream Aida fabric to size,
14 threads/stitches to 2.5cm (1in)
17 × 10.5cm (6¾in × 4¼in) DMC keepsake card
or
Cream Aida fabric to size,
14 threads/stitches to 2.5cm (1in)
7cm (2⅝in) Framecraft frosted-glass trinket bowl

For both:
Stranded cottons in the colours specified in the key

1 Work the cross stitch embroidery centrally on the Aida fabric, using 2 strands of stranded cotton for the cross stitch and 1 strand for the backstitch.

2 Mount the embroidery in the card or trinket bowl following the instructions given on pages 15–16.

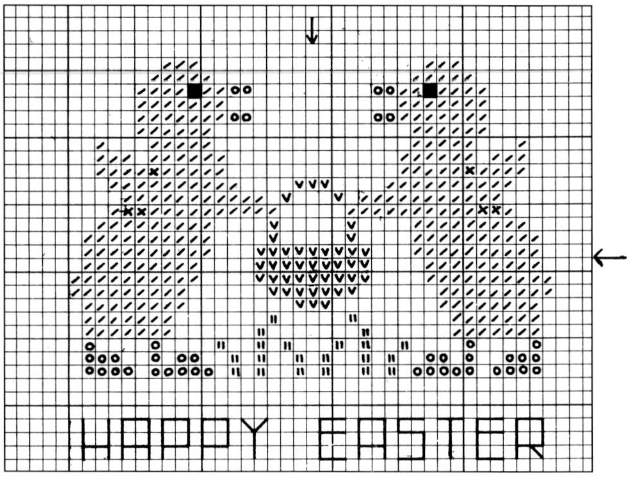

EASTER CHICKS

■	310	Black
⧄	444	Dark lemon yellow
⊠	972	Deep canary yellow
[O]	970	Light pumpkin orange
[II]	911	Medium emerald green
[V]	436	Tan brown
—		**backstitch**
		947 Burnt orange

HAPPY EASTER

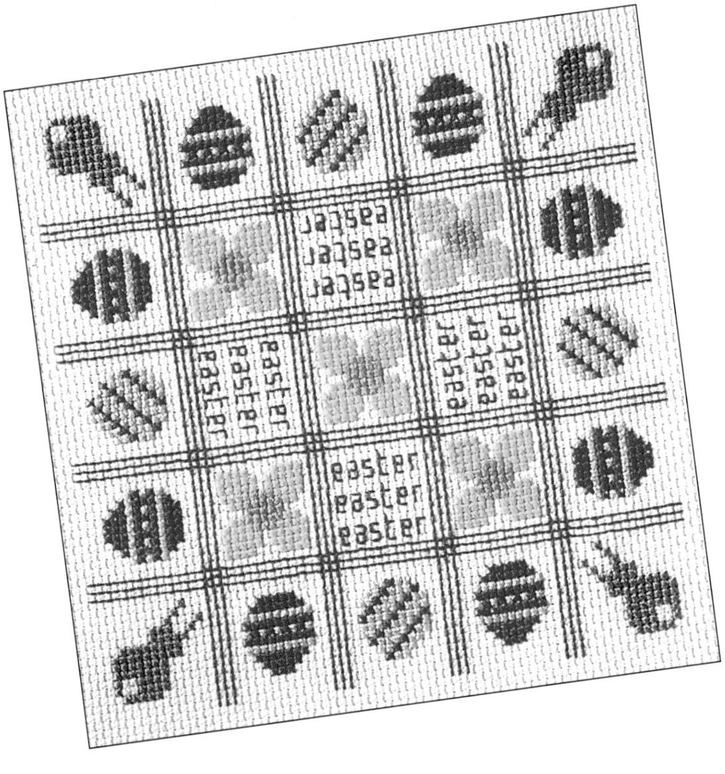

EGGS IN A BASKET

Line your Easter-egg basket with this pretty cloth featuring decorative eggs, daffodils and cute Easter bunnies – and for once put all your eggs in one basket!

YOU WILL NEED

28.5cm (11¼in) square white Aida fabric, 11 threads/stitches to 2.5cm (1in)
Stranded cottons in the colours specified in the key

1 Work the cross stitch embroidery centrally on the Aida fabric using 3 strands of stranded cotton for the cross stitch and 2 strands for the backstitch. Press the completed embroidery if required.
2 To create the frayed edge remove one fabric thread at a time until you have a fringe 1cm (⅜in) deep all the way round.

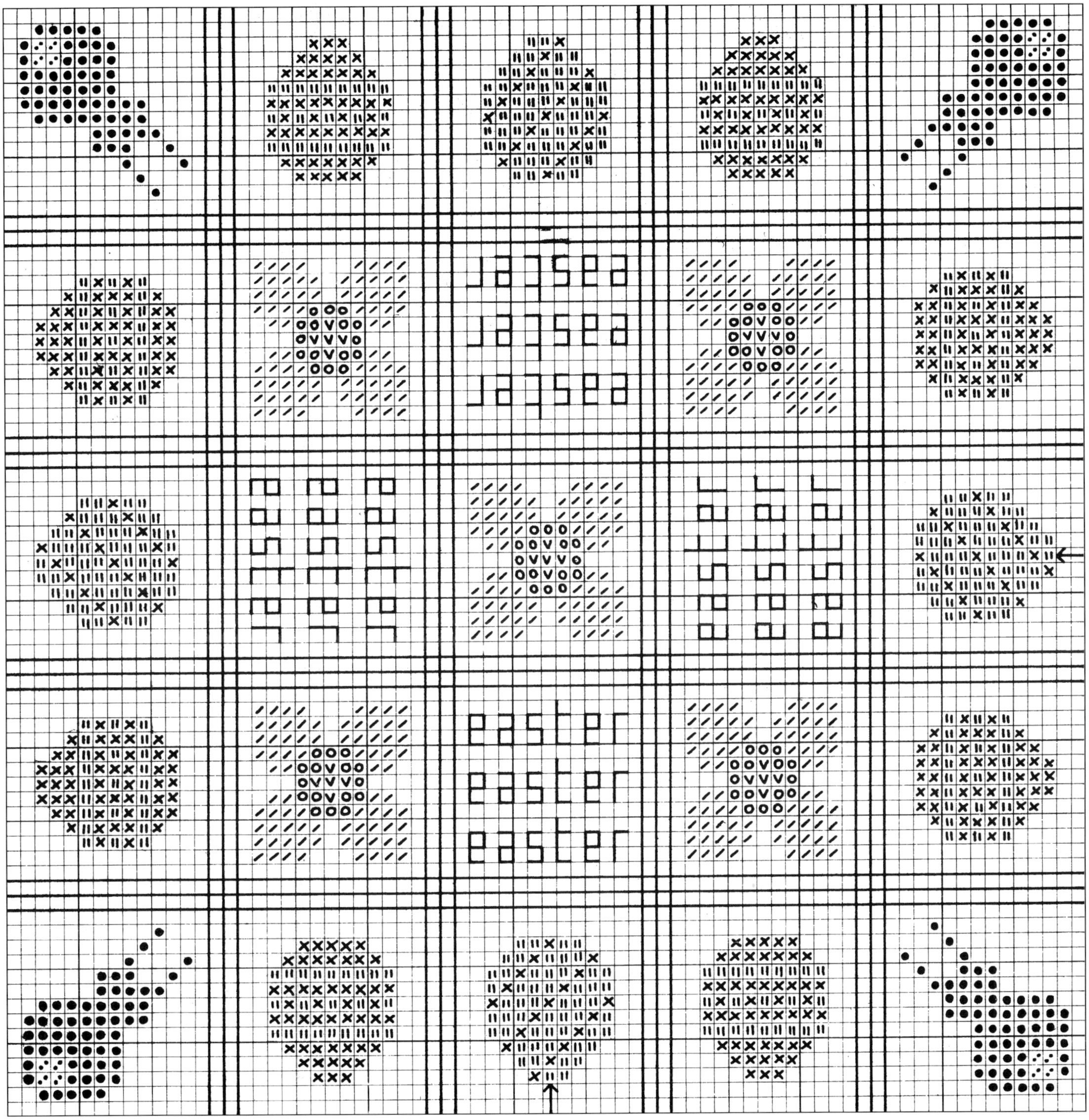

EGGS IN A BASKET

Symbol	No.	Colour
●	435	Very light brown
⁚		White
‖	676	Light old gold
X	601	Dark cranberry
/	444	Dark lemon yellow
O	741	Medium tangerine orange
V	740	Tangerine orange

— **backstitch**
601 Dark cranberry

MOTHER'S DAY

HAPPY MOTHER'S DAY

A pretty little iris and Mother's Day wishes for a card or charming trinket bowl.

YOU WILL NEED

Cream Aida fabric to size,
14 threads/stitches to 2.5cm (1in)
9 × 11.5cm ($3\frac{1}{2} \times 4\frac{1}{2}$in) DMC presentation card
or
White Aida fabric to size,
18 threads/stitches to 2.5cm (1in)
7cm ($2\frac{5}{8}$in) Framecraft gilt trinket bowl

For both:
Stranded cottons in the colours specified in the key

1 Work the cross stitch embroidery centrally on the Aida fabric, using 2 strands of stranded cotton for the cross stitch and 1 strand for the backstitch.
2 Mount the embroidery in the card or trinket bowl following the instructions given on pages 15–16.

MOTHER'S DAY GREETINGS

This floral Mother's Day tribute is complemented perfectly by a simple white presentation card. Alternatively, the spray of flowers can be mounted in the lid of a circular handbag mirror.

YOU WILL NEED

Cream Aida fabric to size,
14 threads/stitches to 2.5cm (1in)
15.5 × 11cm (6 × $4\frac{1}{4}$in) DMC presentation card
or
White Aida fabric to size,
18 threads/stitches to 2.5cm (1in)
7cm ($2\frac{5}{8}$in) Framecraft circular handbag mirror

For both:
Stranded cottons in the colours specified in the key

1 Work the cross stitch embroidery centrally on the Aida fabric, using 2 strands of stranded cotton for the cross stitch and 1 strand for the backstitch.
2 Mount the embroidery in the card or mirror following the instructions given for the card on page 15 and, for the mirror, for trinket bowls on page 16.

HAPPY MOTHER'S DAY

⧄	**208**	Very dark lavender
☒	**307**	Lemon yellow
⊞	**912**	Light emerald green
—		**backstitch**
		208 Very dark lavender

MOTHER'S DAY GREETINGS

⧄	**899**	Medium pink
⊞	**309**	Deep rose red
⊡	**797**	Royal blue
☒	**911**	Medium emerald green
—		**backstitch**
		309 Deep rose red

Happy
Mothers
Day
HAPPY
MOTHERS
DAY

HAPPY
MOTHERS
DAY

RIBBONS AND FLOWERS

Make Mother's Day really special by taking the time to create this beautiful framed picture incorporating ribbons and flowers in sophisticated colours. Complete this attractive gift by choosing a suitable frame.

YOU WILL NEED

33 cm (13 in) square lemon Aida fabric,
14 threads/stitches to 2.5cm (1 in)
Stranded cottons and Kreinik blending filament in the colours specified in the key
25.5 cm (10in) square mounting board
Masking tape
Picture frame of your choice

RIBBONS AND FLOWERS

◪	**349**	Red + 003HL-BF
‖	**350**	Light red
◎	**743**	Dark yellow
V	**700**	Bright Christmas green
X	**989**	Light forest green
–		**backstitch**
	310	Black

1 Work the cross stitch embroidery centrally on the Aida fabric, using 2 strands of stranded cotton for the cross stitch and incorporating the Kreinik blending filaments as indicated and 1 strand for the backstitch.
2 Mount the embroidery on the mounting board following the instructions given on page 14. Your picture is now ready for framing.

HEARTS IN CLOVER

Hearts and lucky four-leaved clover bring good wishes for Mother's Day, to make up into a delightful keepsake gift.

YOU WILL NEED

White Aida fabric to size,
18 threads/stitches to 2.5cm (1in)
7.5cm (2⅞in) Framecraft circular domed paperweight
or
Cream Aida fabric to size,
14 threads/stitches to 2.5cm (1in)
8cm (3¼in) DMC circular frame

For both:
Stranded cottons in the colours specified in the key

1 Work the cross stitch embroidery centrally on the Aida fabric, using 2 strands of stranded cotton for the cross stitch and 1 strand for the backstitch.

2 Mount the embroidery in the paperweight or frame following the instructions on pages 16–17.

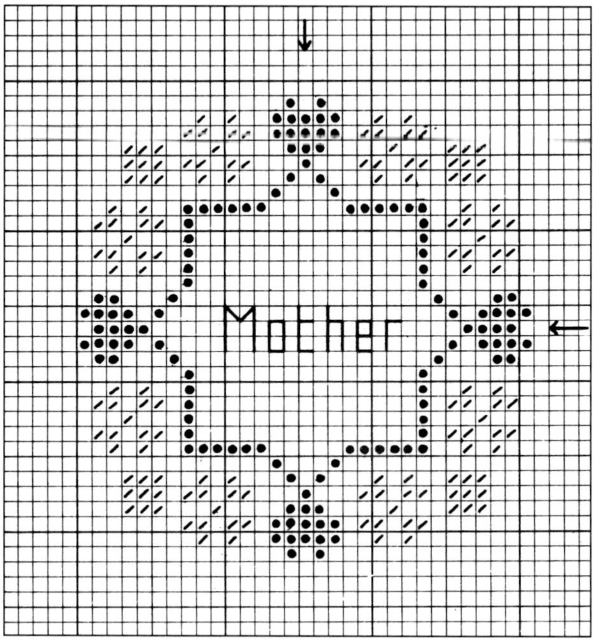

HEARTS IN CLOVER

●	**666**	Bright Christmas red
⁄	**911**	Medium emerald green
–		**backstitch**
	666	Bright Christmas red

*F*ATHER'S DAY

HOME IMPROVEMENT

For the handyman – this Father's Day card is stitched in muted woodworking colours, set off by the strong toning shade used for the formal presentation card.

YOU WILL NEED

Sky blue Aida fabric to size,
14 threads/stitches to 2.5cm (1in)
Stranded cottons in the colours specified in the key
9 × 11.5cm (3½ × 4½in) DMC presentation card

1 Work the cross stitch embroidery centrally on the Aida fabric, using 2 strands of stranded cotton for the cross stitch and 1 strand for the backstitch.
2 Mount the embroidery in the card following the instructions given on page 15.

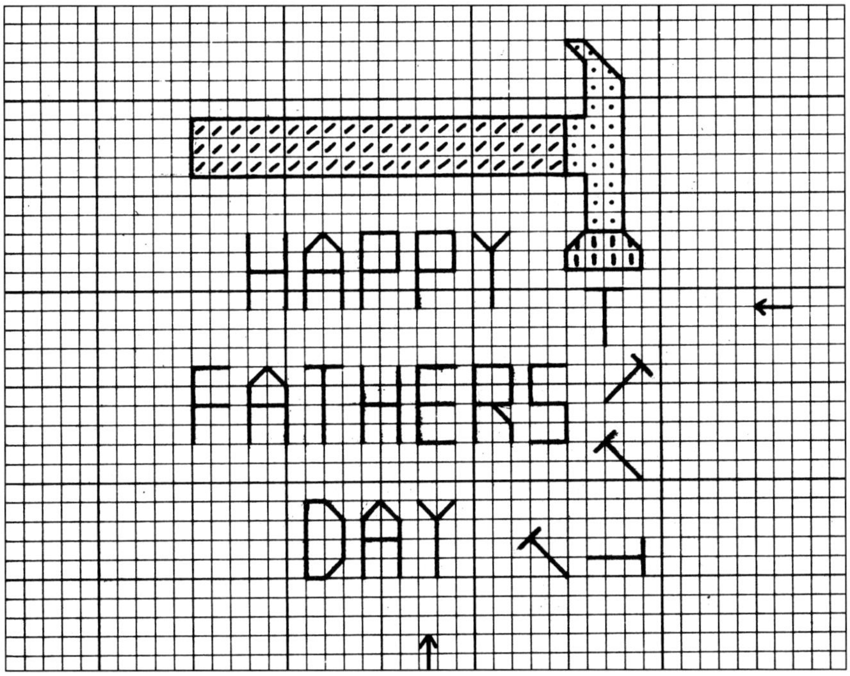

HOME IMPROVEMENT

◪	**436**	Tan brown
⊡	**414**	Steel grey
⎕	**415**	Pale grey
–		**backstitch**
		310 Black

GARDEN DAYS

If your father is a keen gardener, this handsome card would be an ideal way in which to wish him 'Happy Father's Day'.

YOU WILL NEED

Sky blue Aida fabric to size,
14 threads/stitches to 2.5cm (1in)
Stranded cottons in the colours specified in the key
9 × 11.5cm (3½ × 4½in) DMC presentation card

1 Work the cross stitch embroidery centrally on the Aida fabric, using 2 strands of stranded cotton for the cross stitch and 1 strand for the backstitch.
2 Mount the embroidery in the card following the instructions given on page 15.

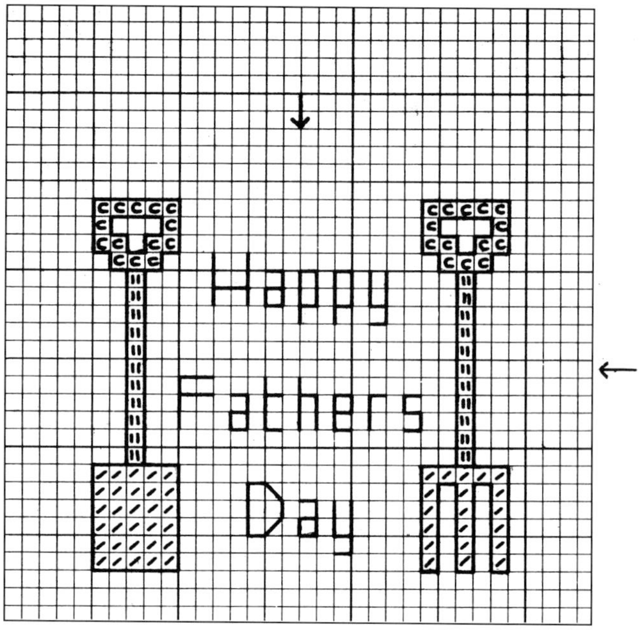

GARDEN DAYS

C	**561**	Dark aqua blue-green
II	**436**	Tan brown
⁄	**414**	Steel grey
–		**backstitch**
		310 Black

TOOLS OF THE TRADE

This Father's Day card, featuring the tools of the trade for the handyman or motor enthusiast, fits neatly into a large presentation card with circular cut-out.

YOU WILL NEED

Sky blue Aida fabric to size,
14 threads/stitches to 2.5cm (1in)
Stranded cottons in the colours specified in the key
15.5 × 11cm (6 × 4¼in) DMC presentation card

1 Work the cross stitch embroidery centrally on the Aida fabric, using 2 strands of stranded cotton for the cross stitch and 1 strand for the backstitch.
2 Mount the embroidery in the card following the instructions given on page 15.

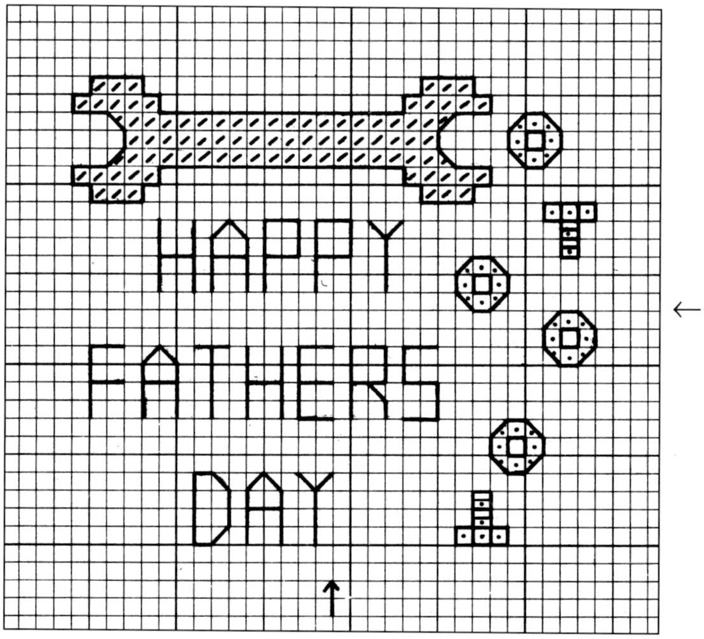

TOOLS OF THE TRADE

⁄	**318**	Light steel grey
•	**414**	Steel grey
–		**backstitch**
		310 Black

Happy
Fathers
Day
HAPPY
FATHERS
DAY
HAPPY
FATHERS
DAY

STEAM DAYS

A classic green steam engine chugs across this Father's Day design, for mounting in a brass frame or trinket bowl.

YOU WILL NEED

Sky blue Aida fabric to size,
14 threads/stitches to 2.5cm (1in)
15cm (6in) Framecraft circular brass frame
or
White Hardanger fabric to size,
22 threads/stitches to 2.5cm (1in)
9cm (3½in) Framecraft wooden trinket bowl

For both:
Stranded cottons in the colours specified in the key

1 Work the cross stitch embroidery centrally on the fabric, using 2 strands of stranded cotton for the cross stitch and 1 strand for the backstitch on Aida, and 1 strand throughout on Hardanger.
2 Mount the embroidery in the frame or trinket bowl following the instructions given on pages 17 and 16.

DAYS AFLOAT

This bright yachting design can be mounted in a brass frame or oval paperweight to create a treasured keepsake.

YOU WILL NEED

Sky blue Aida fabric to size,
14 threads/stitches to 2.5cm (1in)
15cm (6in) Framecraft circular brass frame
or
White Hardanger fabric to size,
22 threads/stitches to 2.5cm (1in)
9 × 6cm (3½ × 2⅜ in) Framecraft oval paperweight

For both:
Stranded cottons in the colours specified in the key

1 Work the cross stitch embroidery centrally on the fabric, using 2 strands of stranded cotton for the cross stitch and 1 strand for the backstitch on Aida, and 1 strand throughout on Hardanger.
2 Mount the embroidery in the frame or paperweight following the instructions given on pages 17 and 16.

STEAM DAYS

⧄	910	Dark emerald green
☒	783	Christmas gold
⊡	310	Black
Ⅱ	666	Bright Christmas red
V	317	Medium steel grey
—		**backstitch**
		666 Bright Christmas red

DAYS AFLOAT

⊡	434	Light brown
⧄	444	Dark lemon yellow
☒	798	Dark Delft blue
Ⅱ	666	Bright Christmas red
O	552	Dark violet
⁘		White
—		**backstitch**
		666 Bright Christmas red

HAPPY
FATHERS DAY
HAPPY
FATHERS DAY
HAPPY
FATHERS DAY
HAPPY
FATHERS DAY

BIRTHDAYS

BIRTHDAY DESK SET

This wooden penholder set would make an impressive birthday gift, personalized with the appropriate sign of the zodiac.

YOU WILL NEED

13cm (5in) square silver-fleck Bellana fabric,
20 threads/stitches to 2.5cm (1in)
Stranded cottons and Kreinik blending filament
in the colours specified in the key
Framecraft wooden penholder desk kit
with 6.5cm (2½in) circular lid

1 Work your chosen zodiac cross stitch embroidery centrally on the Bellana fabric, using 1 strand of stranded cotton throughout and incorporating the Kreinik blending filament as indicated.
2 Mount the embroidery in the lid of the desk kit, following the instructions given for trinket boxes and bowls on page 16.

AQUARIUS ~ THE WATER CARRIER

An attractive paperweight for an Aquarian but any zodiac sign can be used.

YOU WILL NEED

White Hardanger fabric to size,
22 threads/stitches to 2.5cm (1in)
Stranded cottons and Kreinik blending filaments
in the colours specified in the key
6.5cm (2½in) Framecraft scalloped paperweight

1 Work the cross stitch embroidery centrally on the Hardanger fabric, using 1 strand of stranded cotton throughout and incorporating the Kreinik blending filament as indicated.
2 Mount the embroidery in the paperweight following the instructions given on page 16.

ARIES ~ THE RAM

The Aries design is mounted in a pale pink card, which tones perfectly with the embroidery.

YOU WILL NEED

White Aida fabric to size,
14 threads/stitches to 2.5cm (1in)
Stranded cottons and Kreinik blending filaments
in the colours specified in the key
15.5 × 11cm (6 × 4¼in) DMC presentation card

1 Work the cross stitch embroidery centrally on the Aida fabric, using 2 strands of stranded cotton throughout and incorporating the Kreinik blending filament as indicated.
2 Mount the embroidery in the card following the instructions given on page 15.

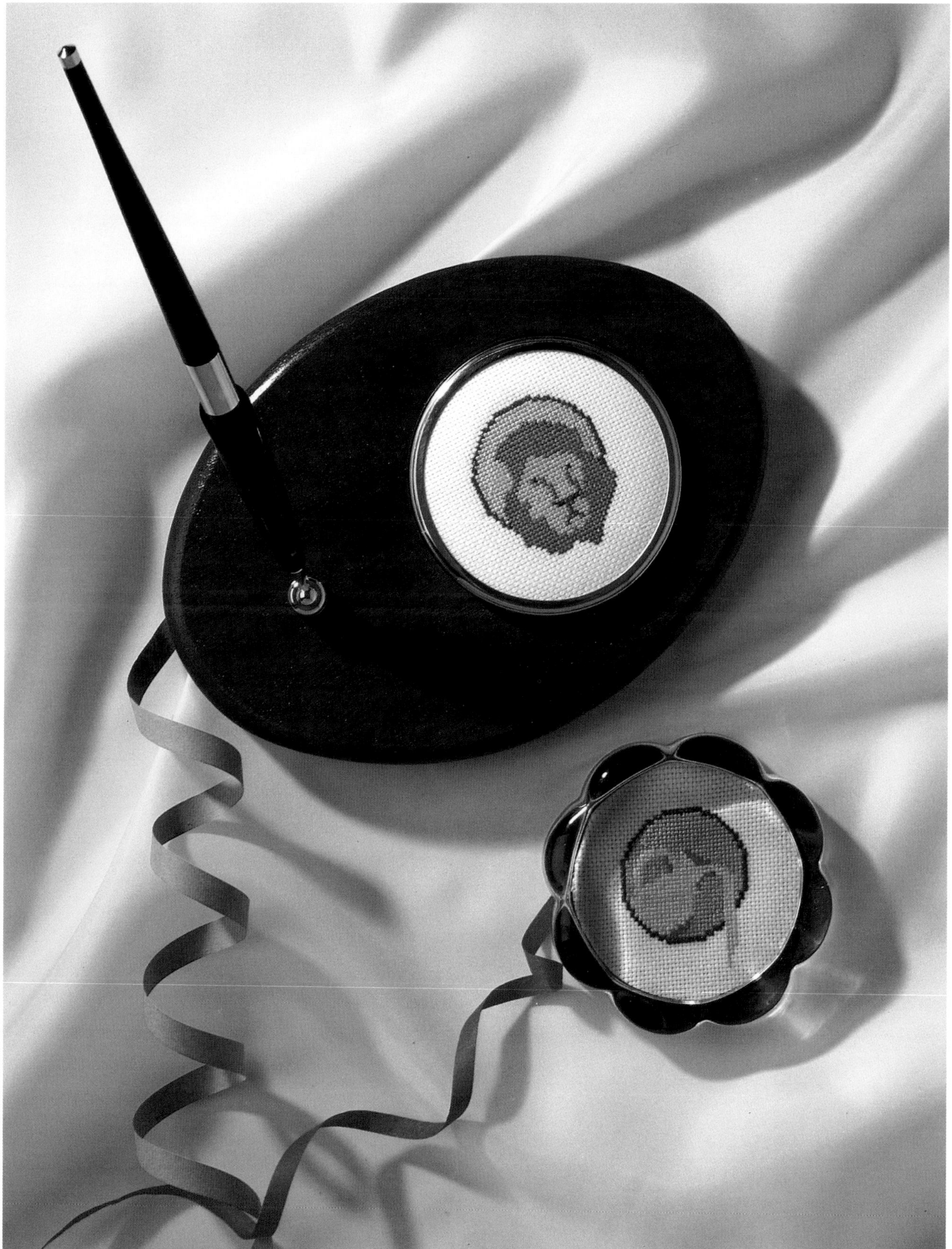

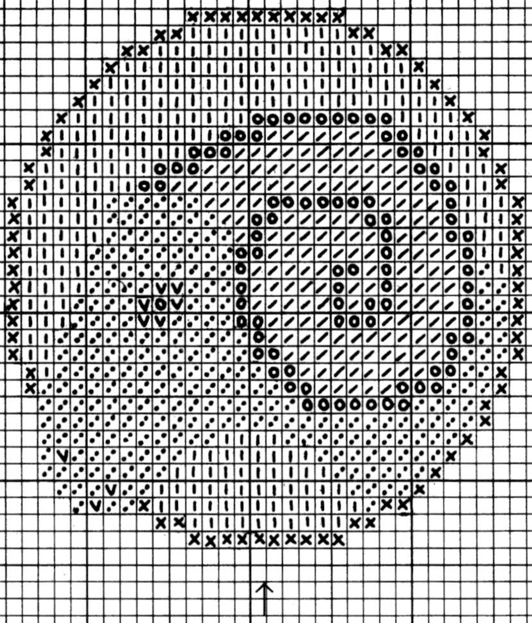

ARIES

SIGNS OF THE ZODIAC

Symbol	Number	Colour
●	550	Very dark violet + 026-BF
◩	554	Light violet
II	600	Very dark cranberry
⁖	964	Light aqua
V	3812	Greenish blue
X	600	Very dark cranberry + 031-BF
O	550	Very dark violet
I	605	Very light cranberry
=	3812	Greenish blue + 014 HL-BF
•		White

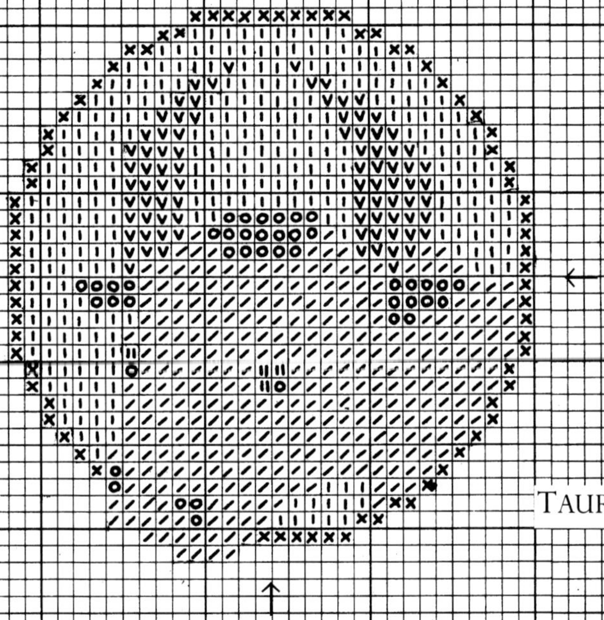

TAURUS

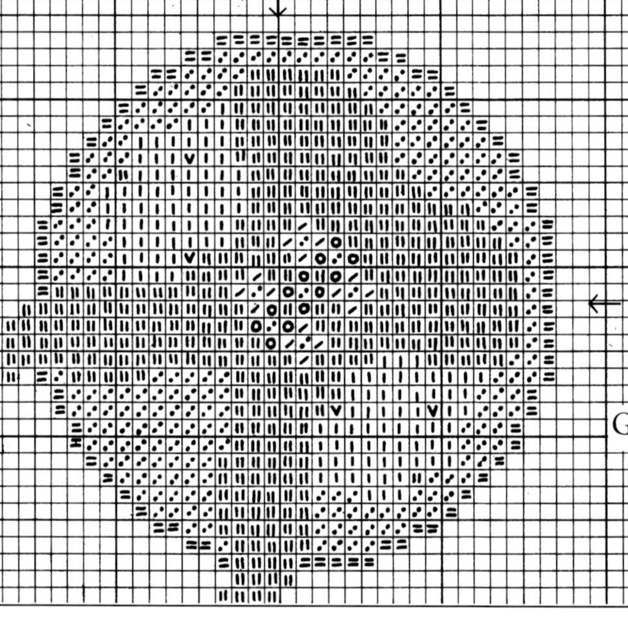

GEMINI

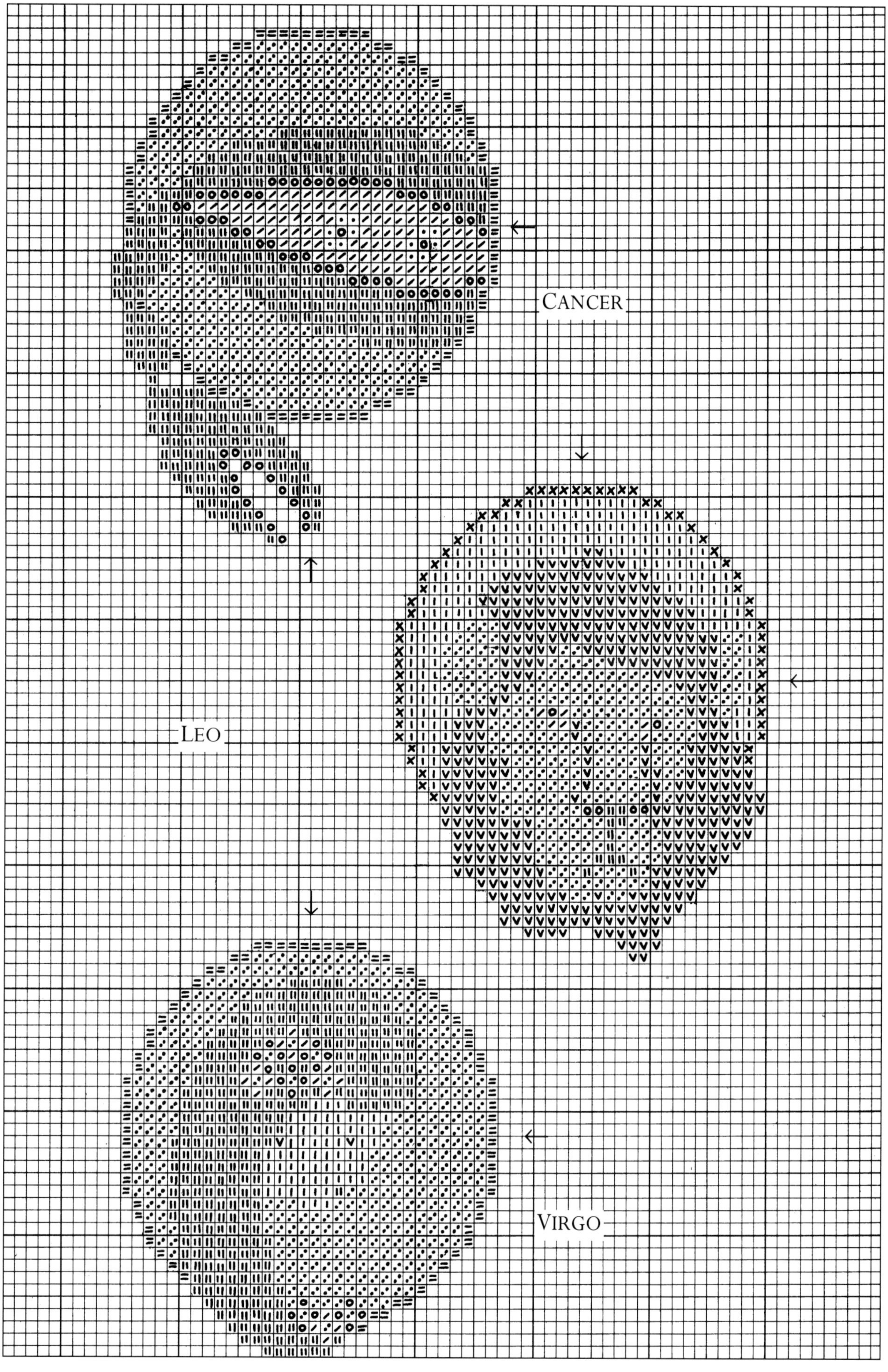
CANCER
LEO
VIRGO

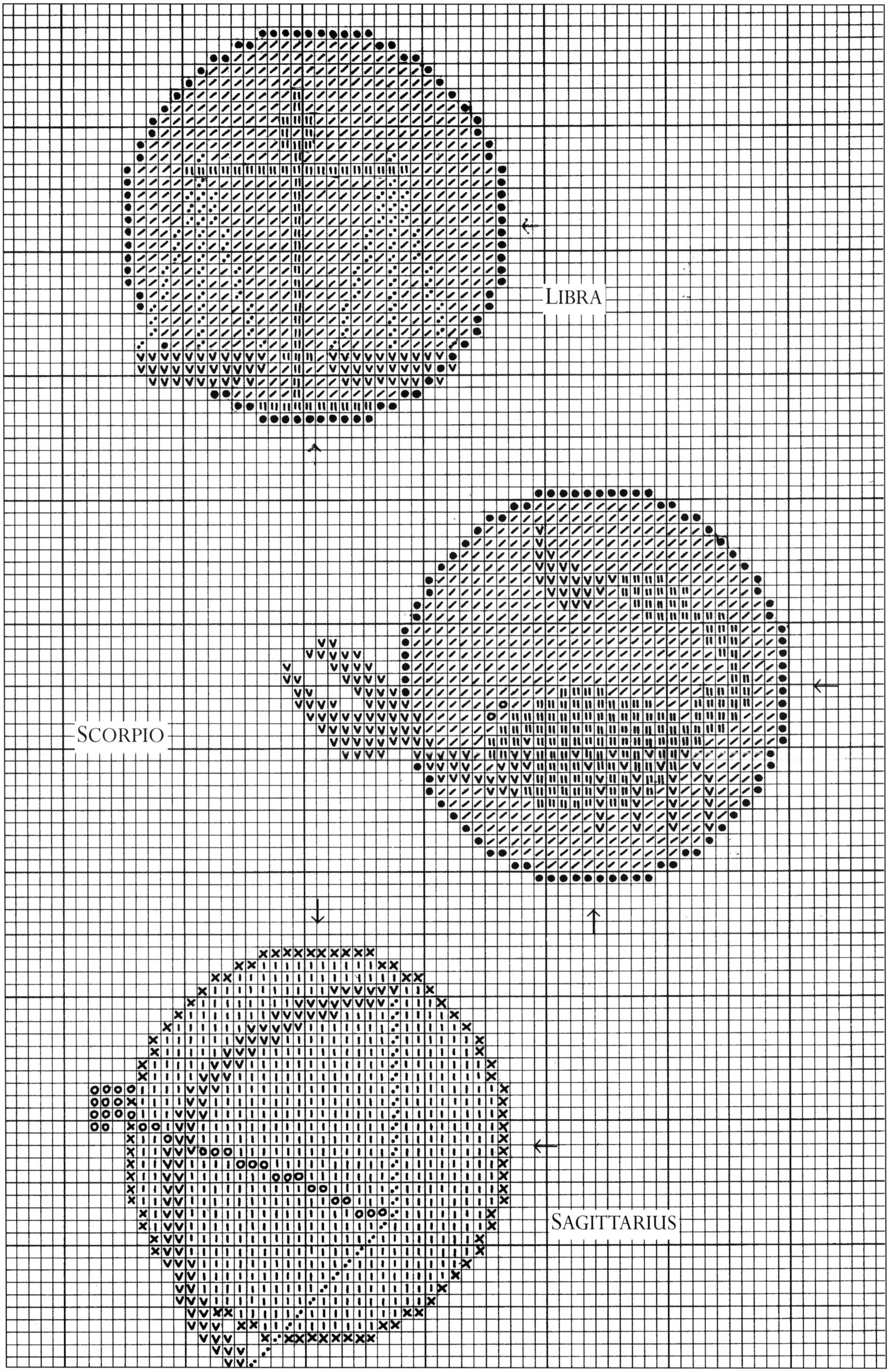
Libra
Scorpio
Sagittarius

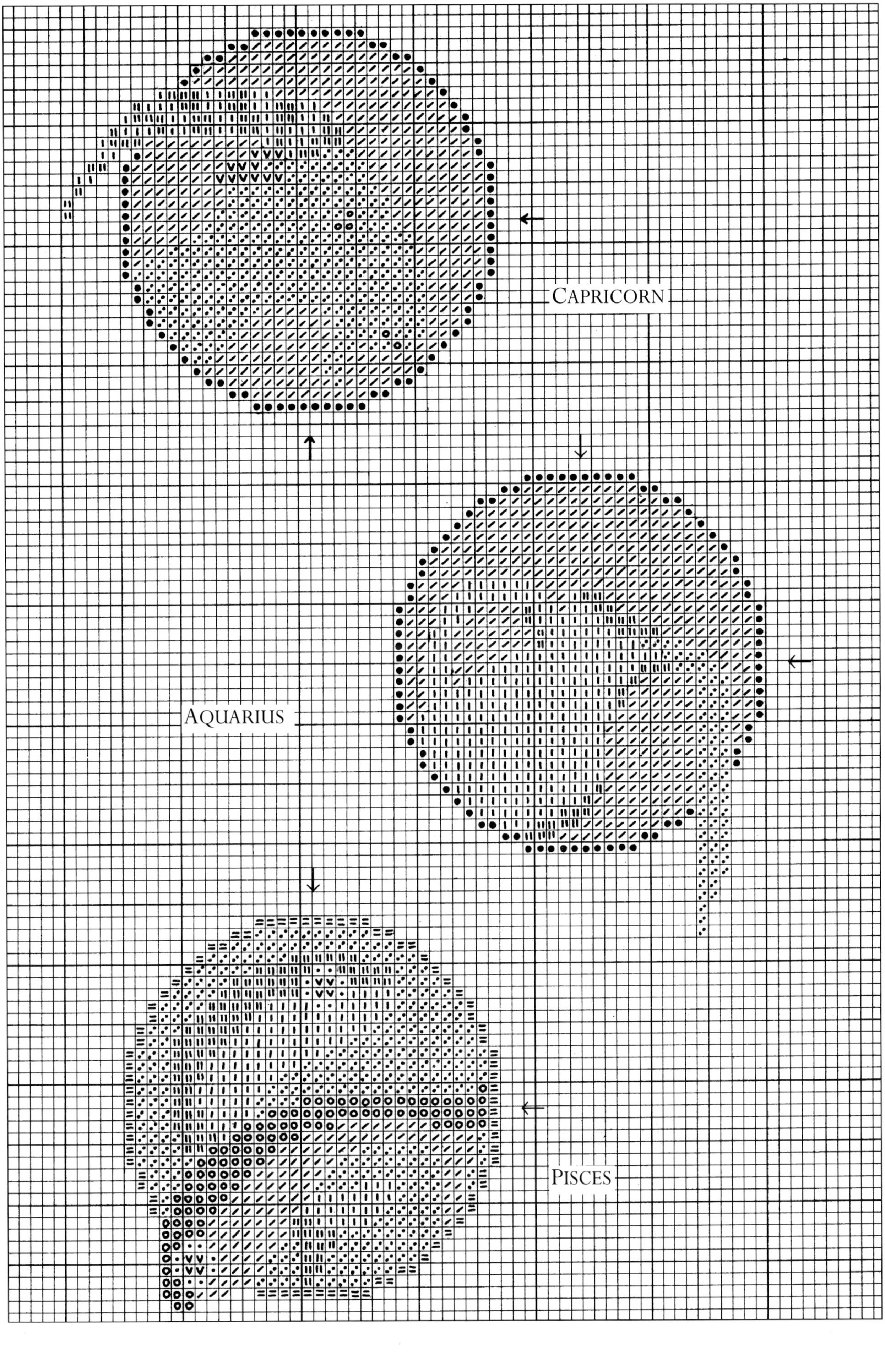
CAPRICORN
AQUARIUS
PISCES

VIRGO ~ THE VIRGIN

This charming Virgo design looks good mounted in a green presentation card, which tones well with the background and border.

YOU WILL NEED

White Aida fabric to size,
14 threads/stitches to 2.5cm (1in)
Stranded cottons and Kreinik blending filaments
in the colours specified in the key
15.5 × 11cm (6 × 4¼in) DMC presentation card

1 Work the cross stitch embroidery centrally on the Aida fabric, using 2 strands of stranded cotton throughout and incorporating the Kreinik blending filament as indicated.
2 Mount the embroidery in the card following the instructions given on page 15.

PISCES ~ THE FISH

The silver-fleck fabric used for the Pisces design is complemented by a sponge-effect pale blue presentation card mount.

YOU WILL NEED

Silver-fleck Bellana fabric to size,
20 threads/stitches to 2.5cm (1in)
Stranded cottons and Kreinik blending filaments
in the colours specified in the key
11.5 × 9cm (4½ × 3½in) DMC presentation card

1 Work the cross stitch embroidery centrally on the Aida fabric, using 1 strand of stranded cotton throughout and incorporating the Kreinik blending filament as indicated.
2 Mount the embroidery in the card following the instructions given on page 15.

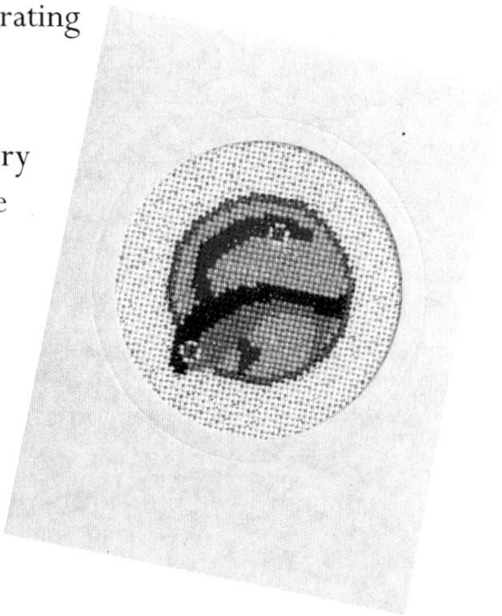

LIBRA ~ THE SCALES

Mount this Libra design in a pale blue presentation card, which complements the muted shades used for the stitching.

YOU WILL NEED

White Aida fabric to size,
14 threads/stitches to 2.5cm (1in)
Stranded cottons and Kreinik blending filaments
in the colours specified in the key
15.5 × 11cm (6 × 4¼in) DMC presentation card

1 Work the cross stitch embroidery centrally on the Aida fabric using 2 strands of stranded cotton throughout and incorporating the Kreinik blending filament as indicated.
2 Mount the embroidery in the card following the instructions given on page 15.

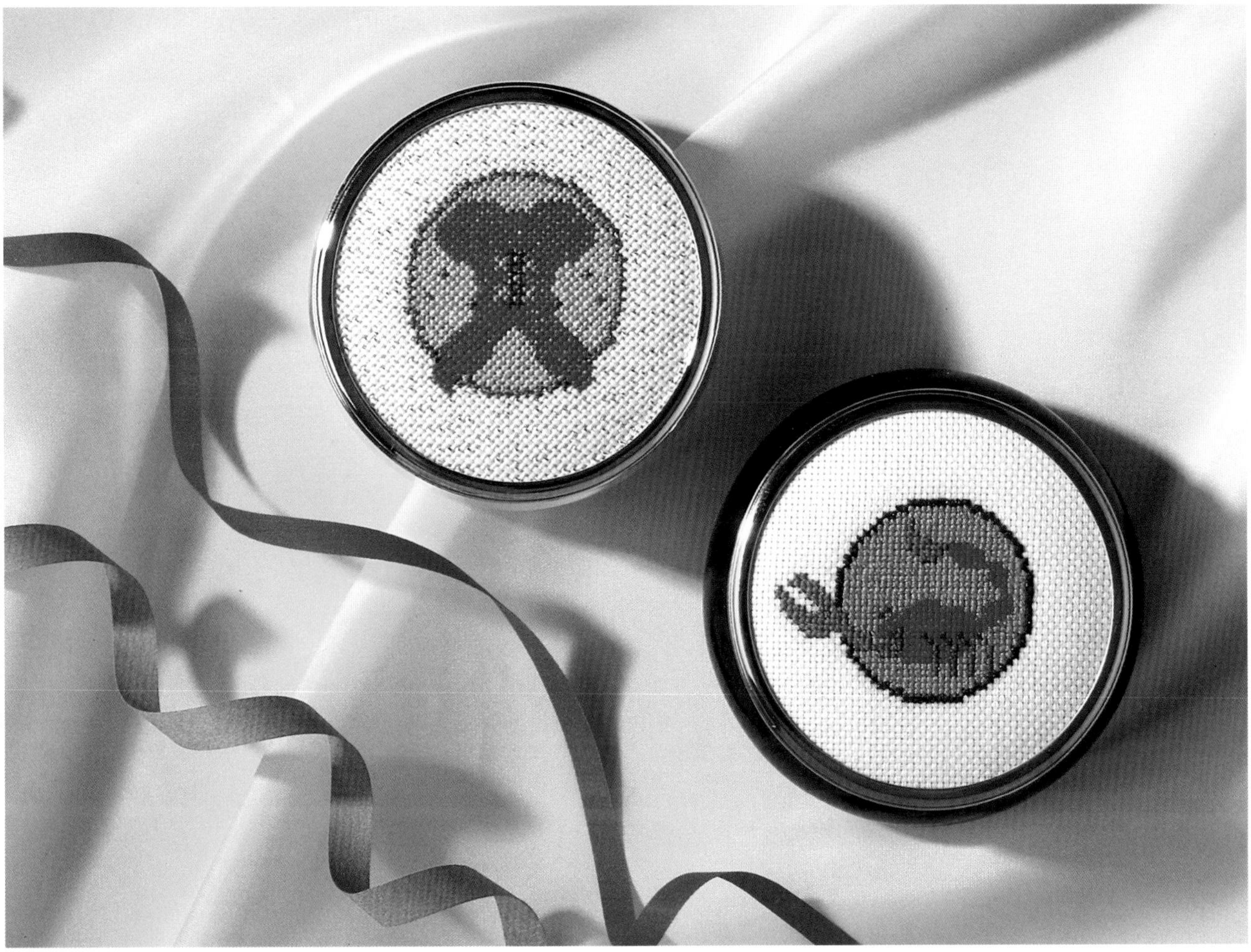

GEMINI ~ THE TWINS

This attractive Gemini design is stitched on silver-fleck fabric, and looks superb mounted in the lid of a miniature silver-plated trinket bowl.

YOU WILL NEED

Silver-fleck Bellana fabric to size, 20 threads/stitches to 2.5cm (1in)
Stranded cottons and Kreinik blending filaments in the colours specified in the key
7cm (2⅞in) Framecraft silver-plated trinket bowl

1 Work the cross stitch embroidery centrally on the Bellana fabric, using 1 strand of stranded cotton throughout and incorporating the Kreinik blending filament as indicated.
2 Mount the embroidery in the trinket bowl following the instructions given on page 16.

SCORPIO ~ THE SCORPION

This Scorpio design is stitched on white fabric, then mounted in a black porcelain bowl to create a striking effect.

YOU WILL NEED

White Hardanger fabric to size, 22 threads/stitches to 2.5cm (1in)
Stranded cottons and Kreinik blending filaments in the colours specified in the key
7cm (2⅞in) Framecraft porcelain trinket bowl

1 Work the cross stitch embroidery centrally on the Hardanger fabric, using 1 strand of stranded cotton throughout and incorporating the Kreinik blending filament as indicated.
2 Mount the embroidery in the trinket bowl following the instructions given on page 16.

SPECIAL BIRTHDAYS

BABY'S FIRST BIRTHDAY

This first birthday card for a baby is mounted in a delightful keepsake card decorated with a crowd of jolly animal favourites.

YOU WILL NEED

White Aida fabric to size,
18 threads/stitches to 2.5cm (1in)
Stranded cottons in the colours specified in the key
18 × 12cm (7¼ × 4¾in) DMC keepsake card

1 Work the cross stitch embroidery centrally on the Aida fabric, using 2 strands of stranded cotton for the cross stitch and 1 strand for the backstitch.
2 Mount the embroidery in the card following the instructions given on page 15.

ONE TODAY

The single candle on this toddler-sized birthday cake celebrates baby becoming 'One Today'.

YOU WILL NEED

White Aida fabric to size,
18 threads/stitches to 2.5cm (1in)
Stranded cottons in the colours specified in the key
18 × 12cm (7¼ × 4¾in) DMC keepsake card

1 Work the cross stitch embroidery centrally on the Aida fabric, using 2 strands of stranded cotton for the cross stitch and 1 strand for the backstitch.
2 Mount the embroidery in the card following the instructions given on page 15.

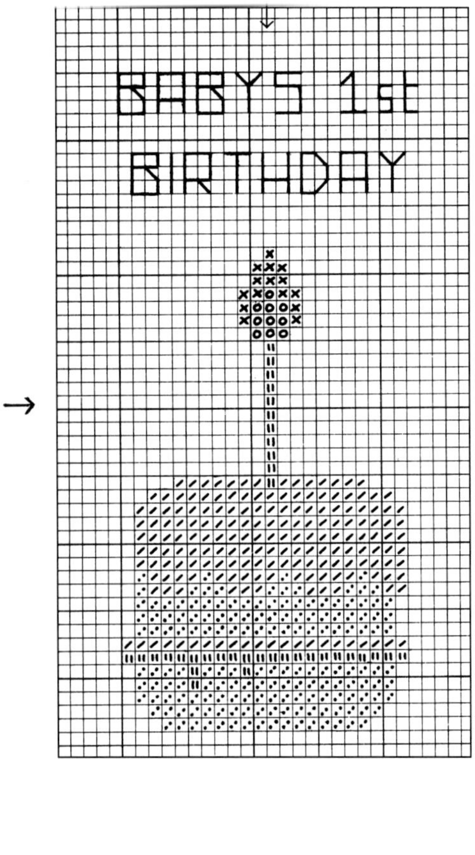

BABY'S FIRST BIRTHDAY

⧄		White
☒	307	Lemon yellow
⌾	972	Deep canary yellow
⊡	437	Light tan brown
⏸	349	Red
–		**backstitch**
		349 Red

ONE TODAY

⧄	605	Very light cranberry
⊡	744	Medium yellow
⏸	437	Light tan brown
●	602	Medium cranberry
V	972	Deep canary yellow
–		**backstitch**
		602 Medium cranberry

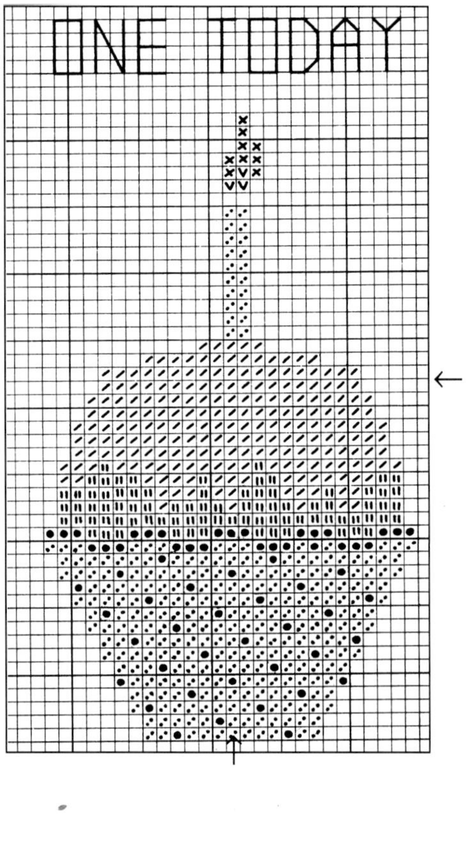

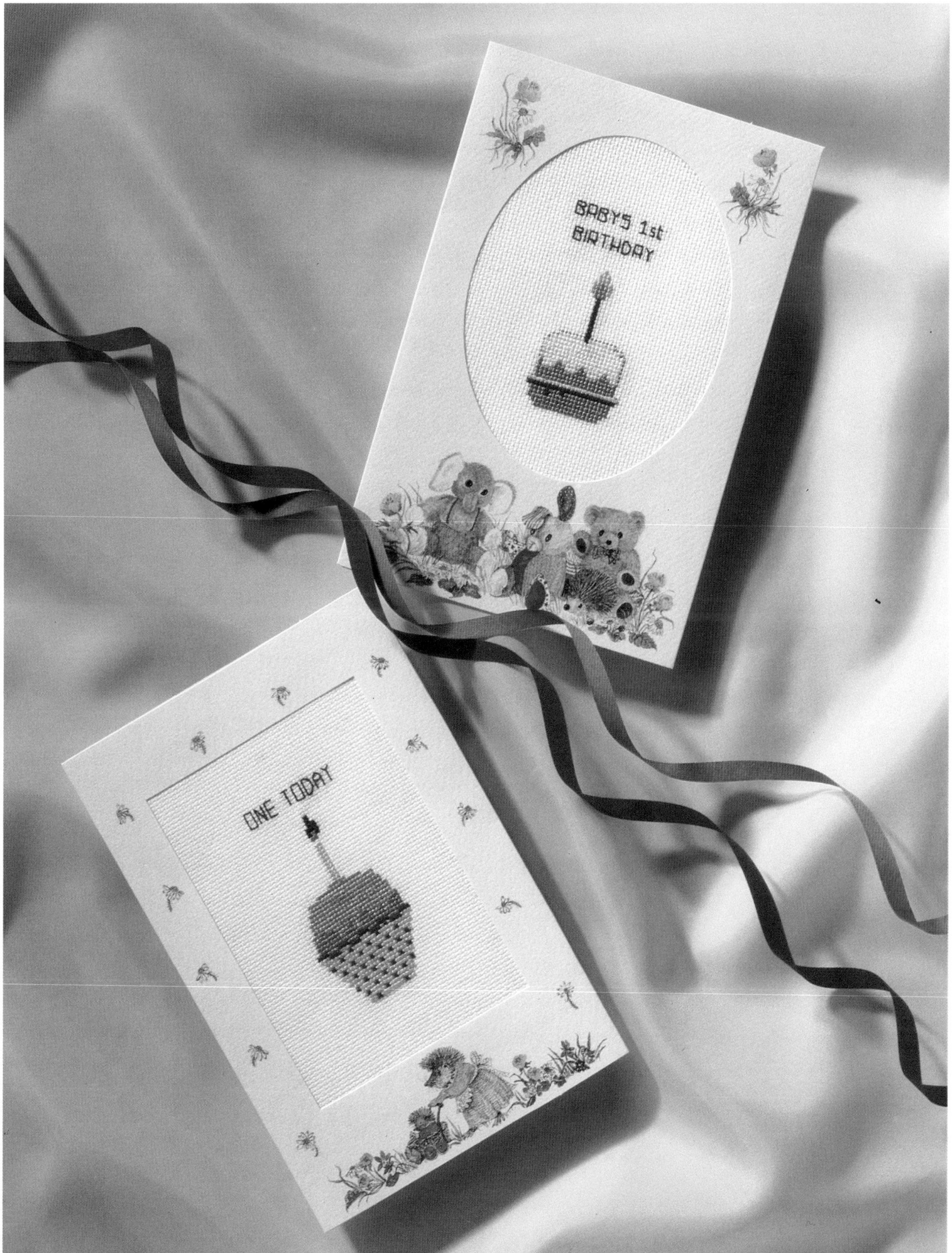
BABY'S 1st
BIRTHDAY
ONE TODAY

HAPPY
BIRTHDAY
HAPPY
BIRTHDAY
SWEET
SIXTEEN

SWEET SIXTEEN

Sixteenth-birthday wishes are surrounded by a selection of confectionery in this unusual design, mounted in an enamel trinket bowl.

YOU WILL NEED

White Aida fabric to size,
18 threads/stitches to 2.5cm (1in)
Stranded cottons and metallic threads in the colours specified in the key
9cm (3½in) Framecraft circular enamel trinket bowl

1 Work the cross stitch embroidery centrally on the Aida fabric, using 2 strands of stranded cotton for the cross stitch and 1 strand for the backstitch, and the metallic threads straight from the reel.

2 Mount the embroidery in the trinket bowl following the instructions given on page 16.

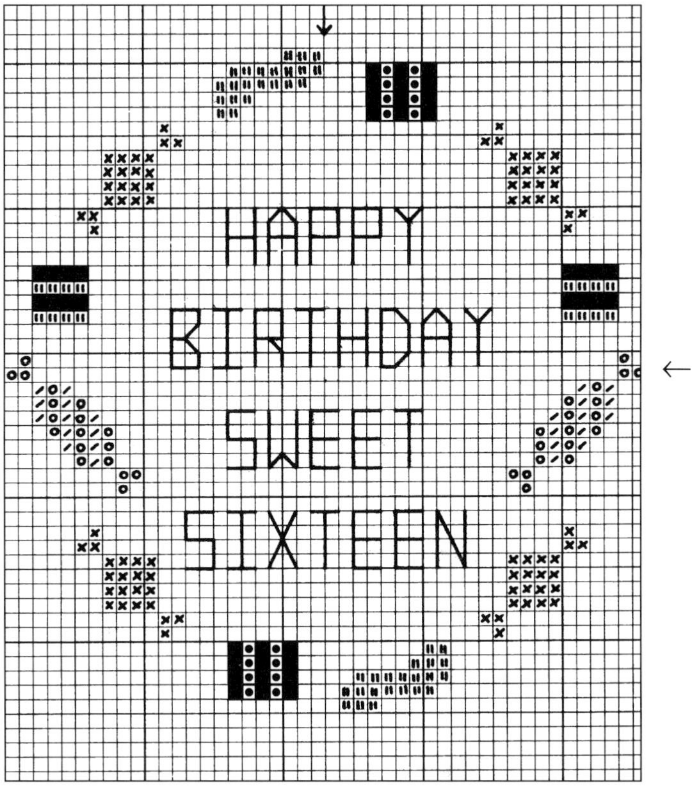

SWEET SIXTEEN

☒		Fil or clair gold thread
■	**310**	Black
◫	**603**	Cranberry
◪	**321**	Christmas red
◎		Fil argent clair silver thread
⊡	**301**	Medium mahogany brown
—		**backstitch**
		799 Medium Delft blue

16 TODAY

Wish a teenager a happy sixteenth birthday with this pretty card decorated with a candy-striped heart design.

YOU WILL NEED

Sky blue Aida fabric to size,
14 threads/stitches to 2.5cm (1in)
Stranded cottons in the colours specified in the key
15.5 × 11cm (6 × 4¼in) DMC presentation card

1 Work the cross stitch embroidery centrally on the Aida fabric, using 2 strands of stranded cotton for the cross stitch and 1 strand for the backstitch.

2 Mount the embroidery in the card following the instructions given on page 15.

16 TODAY

⊡	**899**	Medium pink
◫	**726**	Light topaz yellow
—		**backstitch**
		326 Very deep rose red

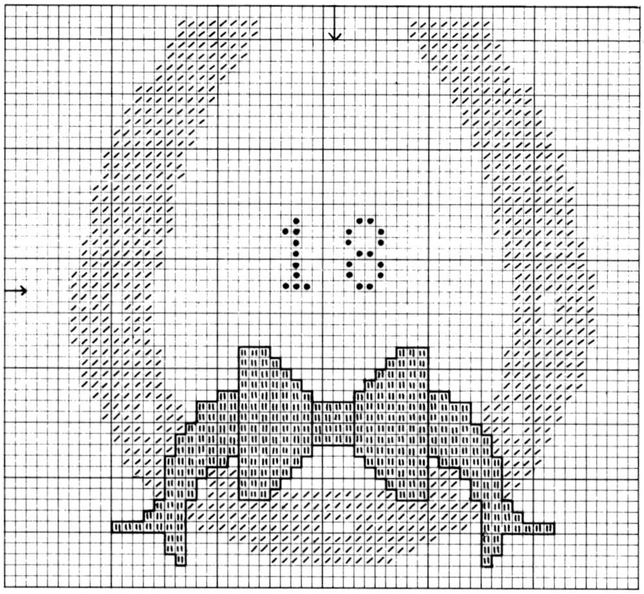

COMING OF AGE

●	**797**	Royal blue
‖	**809**	Delft blue
⧄	**415**	Pale grey + 001-BF
–		**backstitch**
		797 Royal blue

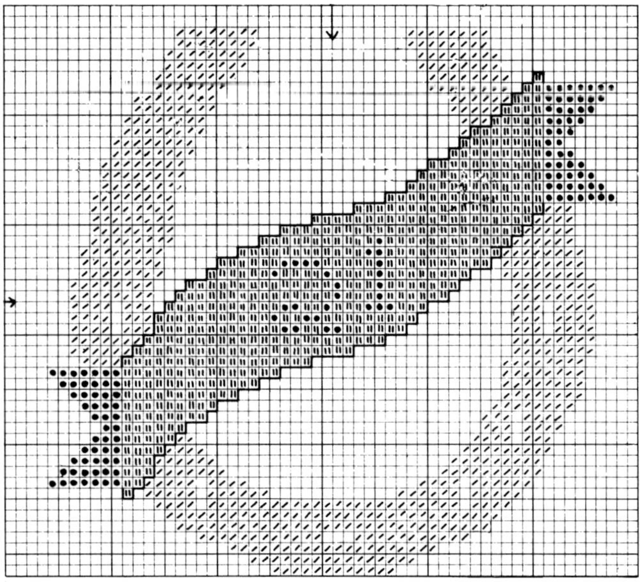

LUCKY 21

●	**602**	Medium cranberry
⧄	**415**	Pale grey + 001-BF
□	**604**	Light cranberry
–		**backstitch**
		602 Medium cranberry

COMING OF AGE

The lucky horseshoe is combined with a blue ribbon bow in this design for an eighteenth birthday.

YOU WILL NEED

White Aida fabric to size,
18 threads/stitches to 2.5cm (1in)
12.5 × 18cm (5 × 7in) DMC presentation card
or
White Aida fabric to size,
14 threads/stitches to 2.5cm (1in)
15cm (6in) Framecraft circular silver-plated frame

For both:
Stranded cottons and Kreinik blending filament in the colours specified in the key

1 Work the cross stitch embroidery centrally on the Aida fabric, using 2 strands of stranded cotton for the cross stitch and incorporating the Kreinik blending filament as indicated, and 1 strand for the backstitch.
2 Mount the embroidery in the card or frame following the instructions given on pages 15 and 17.

LUCKY 21

This lucky horseshoe and ribbon design can be mounted in either an appropriate zodiac card or the lid of a silver-plated frame.

YOU WILL NEED

White Aida fabric to size,
18 threads/stitches to 2.5cm (1in)
18 × 12cm (7¼ × 4¾in) DMC zodiac keepsake card
or
White Aida fabric to size,
14 threads/stitches to 2.5cm (1in)
15cm (6in) Framecraft circular silver-plated frame

For both:
Stranded cottons and Kreinik blending filament in the colours specified in the key

1 Work the cross stitch embroidery centrally on the Aida fabric, using 2 strands of stranded cotton

18
21
18
Aries
21

for the cross stitch and incorporating the Kreinik blending filament as indicated, and 1 strand for the backstitch.

2 Mount the embroidery in the card or frame following the instructions given on pages 15 and 17.

KEY OF THE DOOR

Create these unusual framed pictures featuring the key of the door for a coming of age birthday. You can arrange the cross stitch design, ribbon bow and key as you like, or follow the layouts in the photographs. Alternative key designs are provided, so that your finished picture can be truly unique.

YOU WILL NEED

33 × 28cm (13 × 11 in) white Aida fabric,
14 threads/stitches to 2.5 cm (1in)
Stranded cottons in the colours specified in the key
Blue or pink satin ribbon or ribbon bow
Double-sided adhesive tape
Matching sewing thread
Door key
25.5 × 20.5cm (10 × 8in) mounting board
Masking tape
Picture frame of your choice

1 Work your chosen key cross stitch embroidery in the desired position on the Aida fabric, using 2 strands of stranded cotton for the cross stitch and 1 strand for the backstitch. Remember to allow 4 cm (1½in) all round for mounting.

2 Either make a bow from blue or pink satin ribbon, or buy a ready-made one (available from haberdashery departments and craft shops), and stitch it into position from the wrong side of the fabric, using matching sewing thread and small catch stitches. Fix the ribbon tails into place on the fabric using double-sided adhesive tape.

3 Mount the embroidery on the mounting board following the instructions given on page 14.

4 Fix the key into the desired position, using double-sided adhesive tape or a small dab of adhesive. Your picture is now ready for framing.

KEY OF THE DOOR

⧄	**318**	Light steel grey
◫	**799**	Medium Delft blue
▣	**605**	Very light cranberry

ENGAGEMENT

FLOWERS OF LOVE

A pretty basket of flowers decorates this design for an engagement, mounted in a sponge-effect pastel presentation card.

YOU WILL NEED

Lemon yellow Aida fabric to size,
14 threads/stitches to 2.5cm (1in)
Stranded cottons in the colours specified in the key
11 × 15.5cm (4¼ × 6in) DMC presentation card

1 Work the cross stitch embroidery centrally on the Aida fabric, using 2 strands of stranded cotton for the cross stitch and 1 strand for the backstitch.
2 Mount the embroidery in the card following the instructions given on page 15.

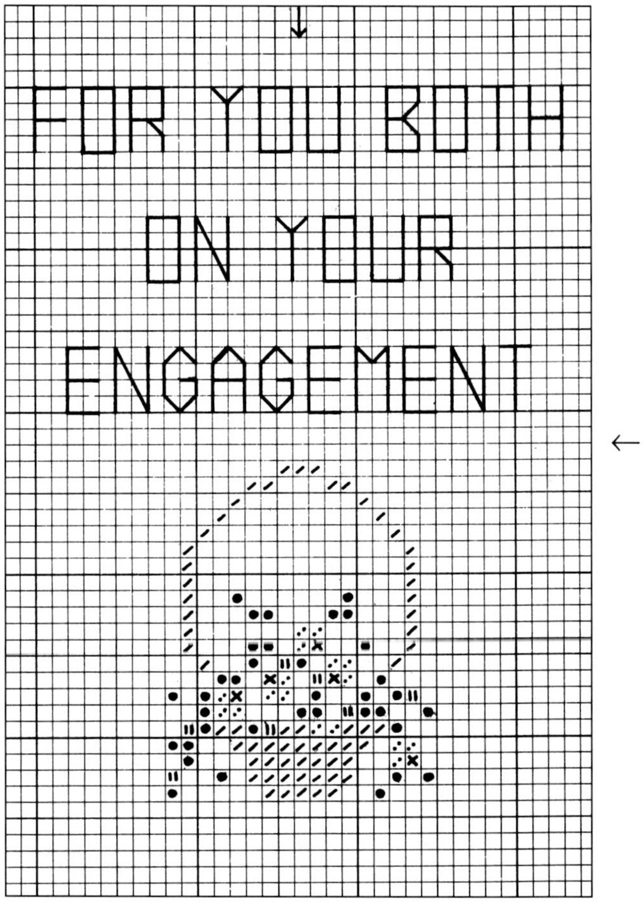

FLOWERS OF LOVE

●	**912**	Light emerald green
‖	**208**	Very dark lavender
X	**602**	Medium cranberry
⁚	**604**	Light cranberry
╱	**436**	Tan brown
–		**backstitch**
		208 Very dark lavender

FOR YOU BOTH
ON YOUR
ENGAGEMENT
GOOD LUCK
JULIE
and
ALAN

LOVE HEARTS

Wish the happy couple good luck on their engagement. Personalize the card using the alphabet provided on page 125.

YOU WILL NEED

Lemon yellow Aida fabric to size,
14 threads/stitches to 2.5cm (1in)
Stranded cottons in the colours specified in the key
11 × 15.5cm (4¼ × 6in) DMC presentation card

1 Work the cross stitch embroidery centrally on the Aida fabric, using 2 strands of stranded cotton for the cross stitch and 1 strand for the backstitch.
2 Mount the embroidery in the card following the instructions given on page 15.

LOVE HEARTS

⊘	**809**	Delft blue
⊞	**604**	Light cranberry
–		**backstitch**
		798 Dark Delft blue

LOVE BIRDS

Congratulate the happy couple with the pretty sampler opposite, personalized using the alphabet provided on page 125.

YOU WILL NEED

38 × 31.5cm (15 × 12½in) white Aida fabric,
14 threads/stitches to 2.5cm (1in)
Stranded cottons and Kreinik blending filament
in the colours specified in the key
30.5 × 24cm (12 × 9½in) mounting board
Masking tape
Picture frame of your choice

1 Work the cross stitch embroidery centrally on the Aida fabric, using 2 strands of stranded cotton for the cross stitch and incorporating the Kreinik blending filament as indicated, and 1 strand for the backstitch.
2 Mount the embroidery on the mounting board following the instructions given on page 14. Your picture is now ready for framing.

LOVE BIRDS

⊘	**318**	Light steel grey + 001-BF
⊠	**415**	Pale grey
⊡		White
⊞	**603**	Cranberry
■	**310**	Black
–		**backstitch**
		lettering **600** Very dark cranberry
		doves **318** Light steel grey
		beaks **977** Golden brown

Congratulations
on your
Engagement
Paul
Jane
26th May 1995

Lucky doves

A pair of white doves bring luck to the happy couple in this charming little design. Mount it in a presentation card in a pastel shade, or in the lid of a pretty cut-glass trinket bowl.

You will need

White Aida fabric to size,
18 threads/stitches to 2.5cm (1in)
11 × 15.5cm (6 × 4¼in) DMC presentation card
or
Sky blue Linda fabric to size,
27 threads/stitches to 2.5cm (1in)
9cm (3½in) Framecraft cut-glass trinket bowl

For both:
Stranded cottons in the colours specified in the key

1 Work the cross stitch embroidery centrally on the fabric, using 2 strands of stranded cotton for the cross stitch and 1 strand for the backstitch on Aida, and 1 strand throughout on Linda.

2 Mount the embroidery in the card or trinket bowl following the instructions given on pages 15–16.

Lucky doves

⊡		White
■	**310**	Black
◪	**783**	Christmas gold
⊞	**809**	Delft blue
—		**backstitch**
		798 Dark Delft blue
		415 Pale grey

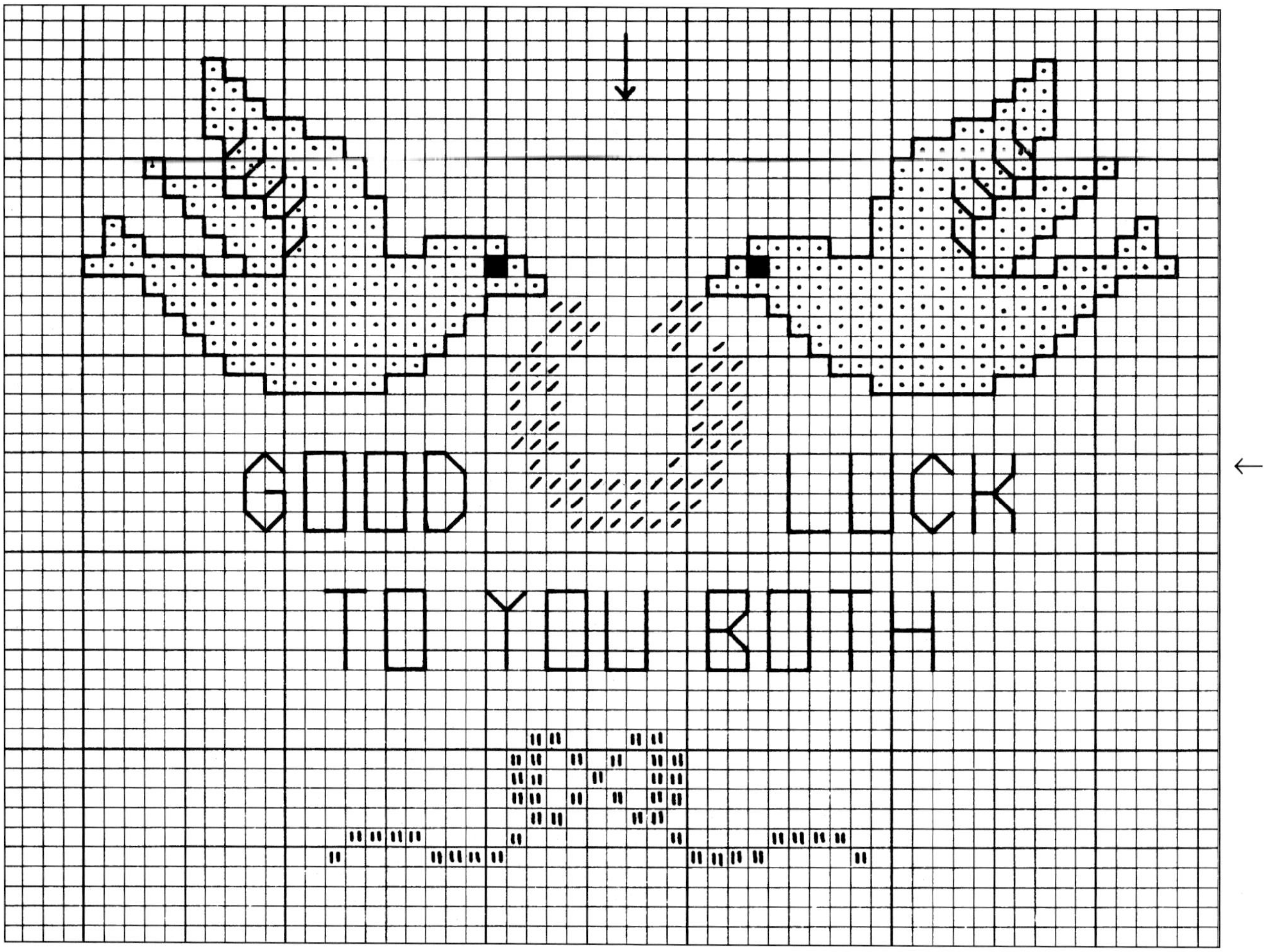

Congratulations
on your
Engagement
Paul
Jane
26th May 1995
GOOD
LUCK
TO YOU BOTH
GOOD
LUCK
TO YOU BOTH

WEDDING DAY

LUCKY HEARTS

Make a lasting gift for the happy couple with this pretty ring pillow, complete with blue and pink satin ribbons.

YOU WILL NEED

28cm (11in) square white Aida fabric,
14 threads/stitches to 2.5cm (1in)
Matching sewing thread
28cm (11in) square contrasting fabric, for backing
Stranded cottons in the colours specified in the key
2m (78 ¾in) pale pink lace, 6cm (2½in) deep
0.5m (19¾in) each pink and blue satin ribbons,
5mm (¼in) wide
25.5cm (10in) square cushion pad

1 Work the cross stitch embroidery centrally on the Aida fabric, using 2 strands of stranded cotton. Press the completed embroidery if required.

2 Place the embroidered fabric face up on a firm, flat surface and pin the lace to the right side. Ensure that the sewing edge of the lace lies just over the stitching line (leave a 1.5cm (½in) seam allowance), with the frill to the centre. Tack carefully, so that the lace is gathered evenly. You may find it helpful to pin the lace to the fabric to keep it away from the seams.

3 Place the backing fabric on the embroidered Aida with right sides together. The lace is now sandwiched between the two fabrics. Pin and tack around three sides. Machine stitch around these three sides.

4 Remove the tacking and turn the pillow cover right side out, releasing the lace frill. Press in the seam allowance on the open edge.

5 Find the centre of your lengths of ribbon and stitch these centrally to the pillow cover, 2.5cm (1in) from the top seam.

6 Insert the cushion pad in the cover, turn in the seam allowance, and oversew the open edge closed by hand.

LUCKY HEARTS

◪	**3078**	Very light golden yellow
◫	**3325**	Baby blue
☒	**963**	Very light dusty rose pink
🅅	**964**	Light aqua

JENNY and ANDREW
St. Marys 19th June 1995

DAY TO REMEMBER

Create a lasting memory with this wedding sampler, personalized using the alphabet provided on page 125.

YOU WILL NEED

38 × 47cm (15 × 18½ in) white Aida fabric, 14 threads/stitches to 2.5cm (1 in)
Stranded cottons and metallic threads in the colours specified in the key
30.5 × 39.5cm (12 × 15½ in) mounting board
Masking tape
Picture frame of your choice

1 Work the cross stitch embroidery centrally on the Aida fabric, using 2 strands of stranded cotton for the cross stitch and 1 strand for the backstitch, and the metallic threads straight from the reel.

2 Mount the embroidery on the mounting board following the instructions given on page 14. Your picture is now ready for framing.

→

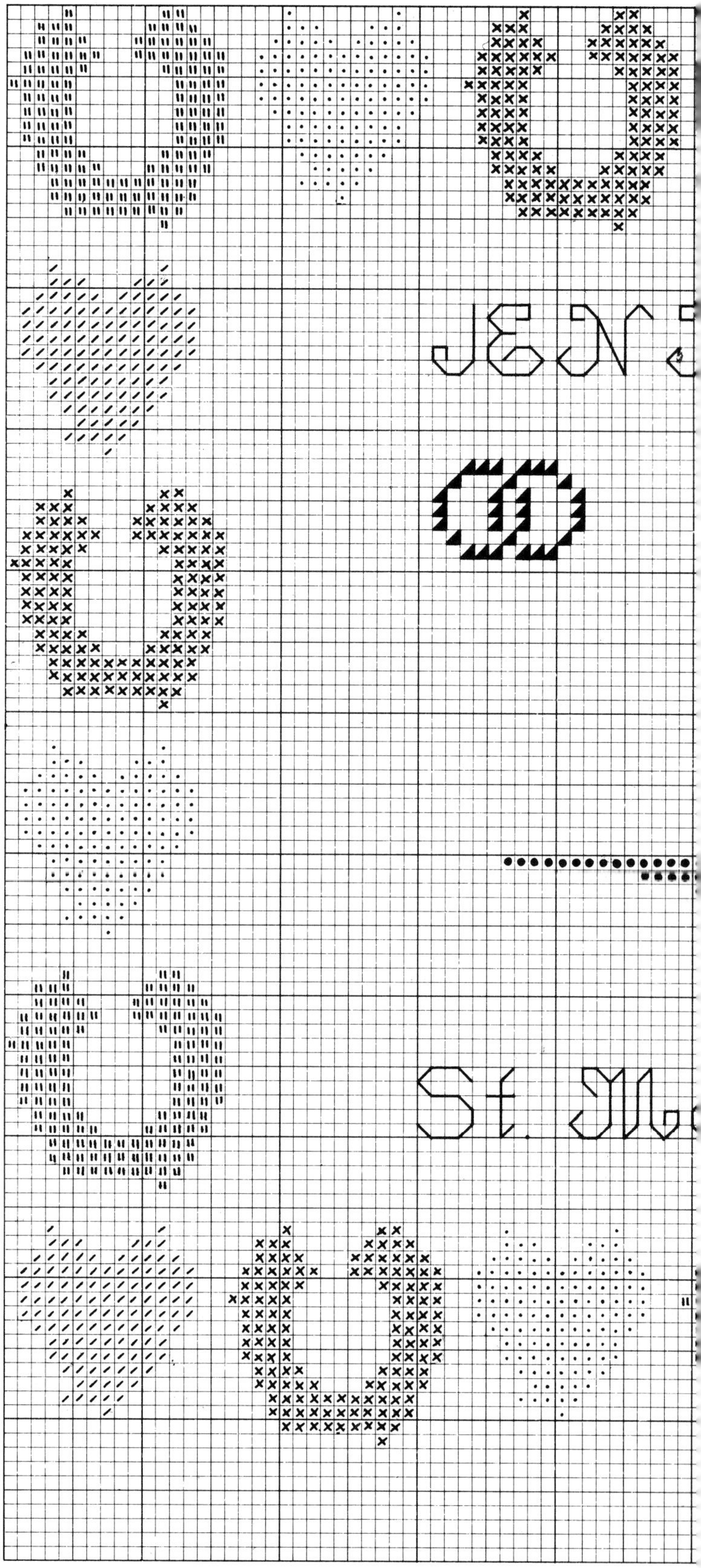

DAY TO REMEMBER

II	3325	Baby blue
╱	3078	Very light golden yellow
Y	444	Dark lemon yellow
•	964	Light aqua
X	963	Very light dusty rose pink
O	970	Light pumpkin orange
◪		Fil or clair gold thread
●	989	Light forest green
■	208	Very dark lavender
⁝	910	Dark emerald green
Z		Fil argent clair silver thread
V	415	Pale grey
=	606	Bright orange-red
N	317	Medium steel grey
C	420	Dark hazelnut brown

– **backstitch**

church and belts	**317**	Medium steel grey
lettering etc	**208**	Very dark lavender

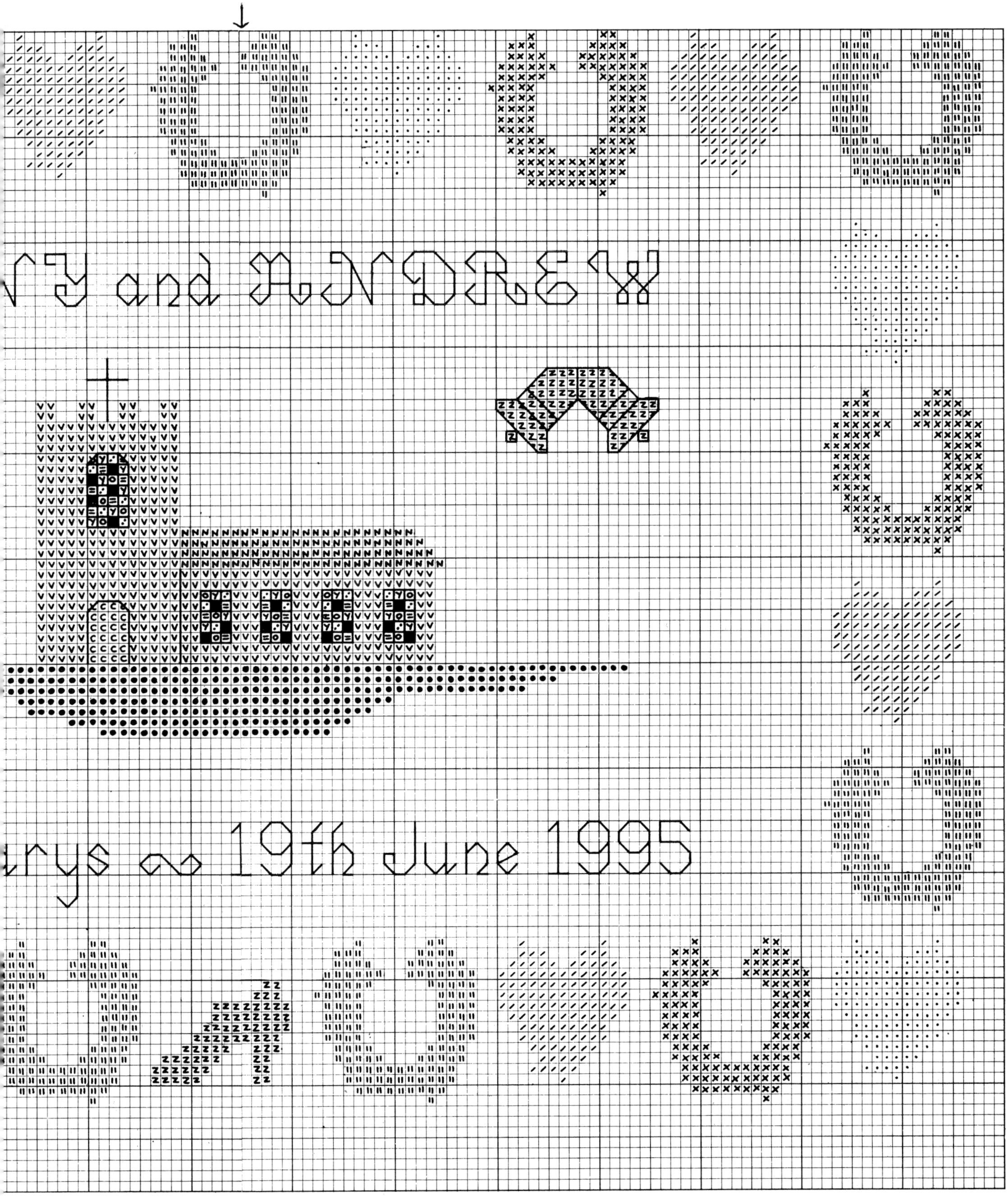
Y and ANDREW
rys 19th June 1995

BRIDE AND GROOM

'Bride' and 'Groom' are worked with shimmery metallic threads in a flowing script, to create this beautiful wedding-day card.

YOU WILL NEED

White Aida fabric to size,
18 threads/stitches to 2.5cm (1in)
Metallic threads in the colours specified in the key
15 × 20cm (6 × 8 in) Framecraft craft card

1 Work the cross stitch embroidery centrally on the Aida fabric, using the metallic threads straight from the reel.

2 Mount the embroidery in the card following the instructions given on page 15.

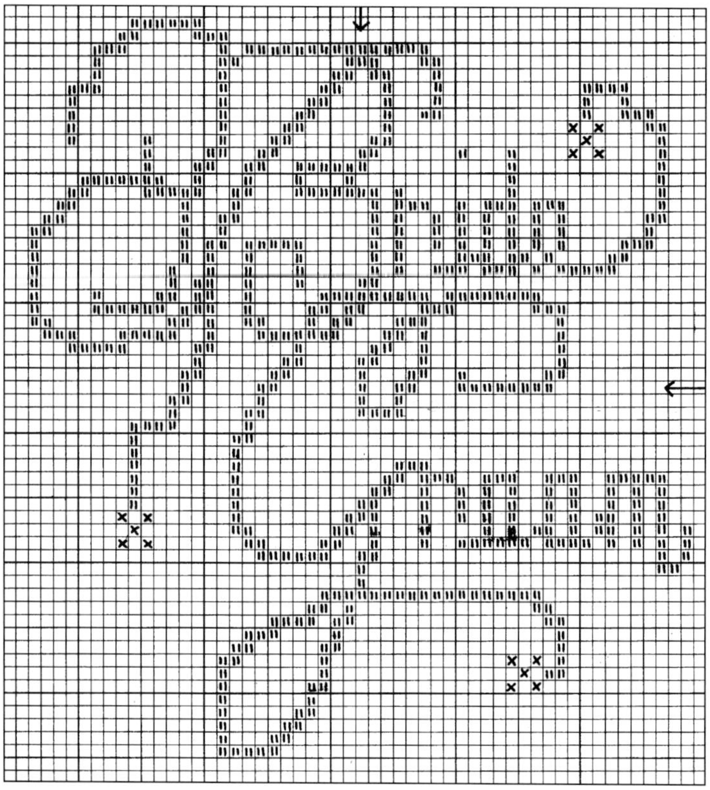

BRIDE AND GROOM

II	Fil argent clair silver thread
X	Fil metallise 4013

SPECIAL DAY

A pretty parasol and top hat displayed in a wedding keepsake card. Alternatively, the design can be made up into a small gift bag.

YOU WILL NEED

White Aida fabric to size,
14 threads/stitches to 2.5cm (1in)
18 × 12cm (7¼ × 4¾in) DMC keepsake card
or
Materials as listed on page 17

For both:
Stranded cottons in the colours specified in the key

1 Work the cross stitch embroidery on the Aida fabric, using 2 strands of stranded cotton for the cross stitch and 1 strand for the backstitch. Position the design centrally on the fabric for the card, and according to the instructions on page 17 for the gift bag.

2 Mount the embroidery in the card following the instructions given on page 15. Alternatively, make it up into a gift bag following the instructions given on page 17.

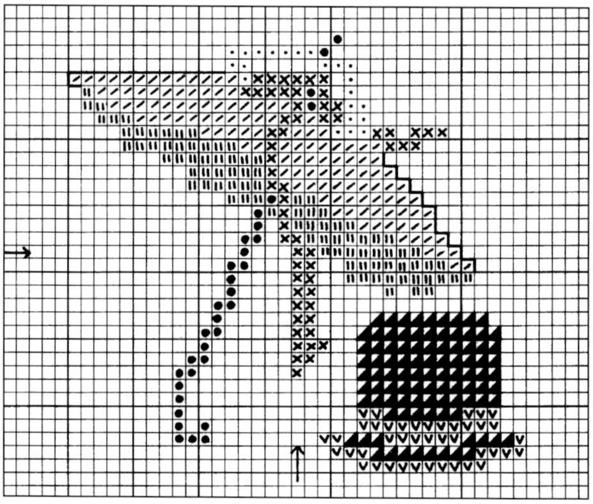

SPECIAL DAY

◩		White
●	**975**	Dark golden brown
◪	**310**	Black
II	**415**	Pale grey
X	**602**	Medium cranberry
•	**605**	Very light cranberry
V	**317**	Medium steel grey
—	**backstitch**	
	318	Light steel grey

Bride
Groom

PAUL and JANE
Congratulations
BEST WISHES
ON YOUR
SPECIAL DAY

BRIDAL BOUQUET

A pretty bridal bouquet in a keepsake card or as decoration on a little gift bag, personalized using the alphabet provided on page 125.

YOU WILL NEED

White Aida fabric to size,
14 threads/stitches to 2.5cm (1in)
18 × 12cm (7¼ × 4¾in) DMC keepsake card
or
Materials as listed on page 17

For both:
Stranded cottons in the colours specified in the key

1 Work the cross stitch embroidery on the Aida fabric, using 2 strands of stranded cotton for the cross stitch and 1 strand for the backstitch. Position the design centrally on the fabric for the card, and according to the instructions on page 17 for the gift bag.
2 Mount the embroidery in the card following the instructions given on page 15. Alternatively, make it up into a gift bag following the instructions given on page 17.

WEDDING RINGS

Quick and easy to stitch, this simple but effective design is mounted in a special wedding-day card.

YOU WILL NEED

White Aida fabric to size,
14 threads/stitches to 2.5cm (1in)
Stranded cotton and metallic thread in the colours specified in the key
20 × 15cm (8 × 6in) DMC keepsake card

1 Work the cross stitch embroidery centrally on the Aida fabric, using 1 strand of cotton for the backstitch and the metallic thread straight from the reel.
2 Mount the embroidery in the card following the instructions given on page 15.

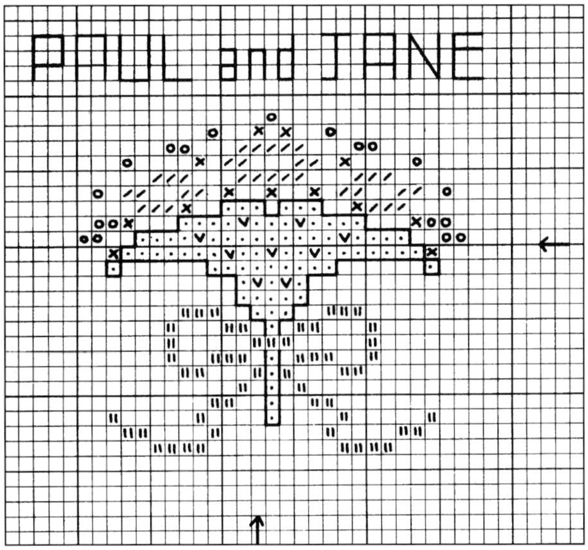

BRIDAL BOUQUET

II	**809**	Delft blue
V	**415**	Pale grey
•		White
/	**604**	Light cranberry
X	**726**	Light topaz yellow
O	**912**	Light emerald green

— **backstitch**
lettering **798** Dark Delft blue
bouquet **415** Pale grey

WEDDING RINGS

X	Fil or clair gold thread

— **backstitch**
356 Medium brick red

WEDDING ANNIVERSARIES

5 YEARS ~ WOOD

A circle of hearts decorates the lid of a circular wooden bowl – the perfect gift for a 5th wedding anniversary.

YOU WILL NEED

White Aida fabric to size,
18 threads/stitches to 2.5cm (1in)
Stranded cotton in the colour specified in the key
7cm (2⅝ in) Framecraft wooden trinket bowl

1 Work the cross stitch embroidery centrally on the Aida fabric, using 2 strands of stranded cotton for the cross stitch and 1 strand for the backstitch.
2 Mount the embroidery in the trinket bowl following the instructions given on page 16.

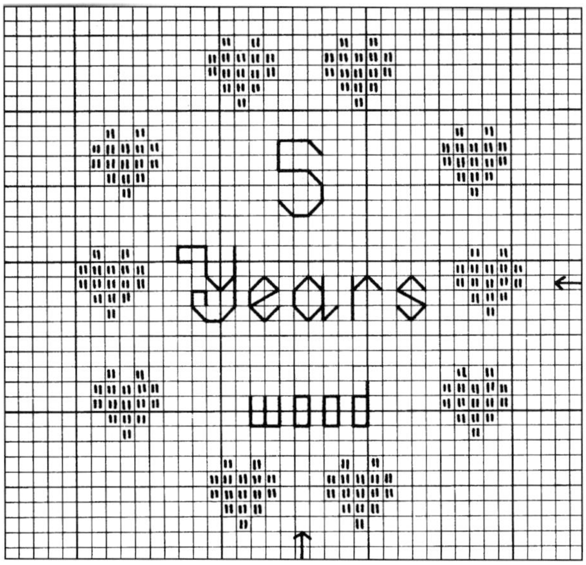

5 YEARS ~ WOOD

▥	**436**	Tan brown
–		**backstitch**
		436 Tan brown

50 YEARS ~ GOLD

The same circle of hearts, worked here in gold metallic thread, has been used in this 50th anniversary design.

YOU WILL NEED

White Aida fabric to size,
18 threads / stitches to 2.5cm (1in)
Metallic thread in the colour specified in the key
7cm (2⅝ in) Framecraft gilt trinket bowl

1 Work the cross stitch embroidery centrally on the Aida fabric, using the metallic thread straight from the reel.
2 Mount the embroidery in the trinket bowl following the instructions given on page 16.

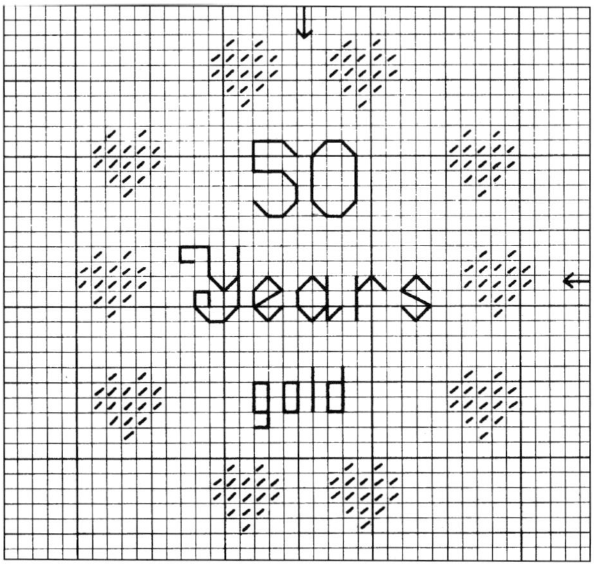

50 YEARS ~ GOLD

◿	Fil or clair gold thread
–	**backstitch**
	Fil or clair gold thread

25
SILVER
30
Years
gold
PEARL
30
5
Years
wood

25 YEARS ~ SILVER

Numbers and letters from the charts on pages 124 and 125 have been combined to create this striking silver-wedding design.

YOU WILL NEED

Navy blue Aida fabric to size,
14 threads/stitches to 2.5cm (1in)
Stranded cotton and Kreinik blending filament
in the colours specified in the key
Assorted beads and trimmings
15cm (6in) DMC circular flexi-hoop

1 Work the cross stitch embroidery centrally on the Aida fabric, using 2 strands of stranded cotton for the cross stitch and 1 strand for the backstitch, and incorporating the Kreinik blending filament as indicated.

2 Mount the embroidery in the flexi-hoop following the instructions given on page 15.

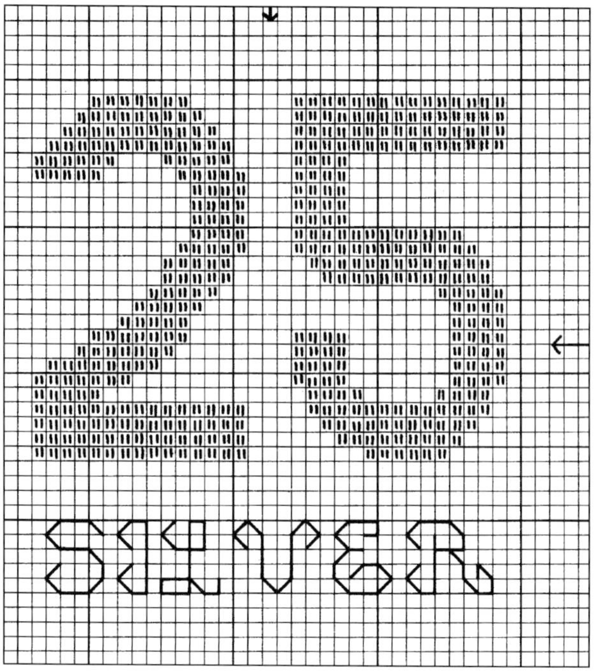

25 YEARS ~ SILVER

▥	**415**	Pale grey + 001-BF
—		**backstitch**
		415 Pale grey + 001-BF

30 YEARS ~ PEARL

Pearly trimmings, including butterflies and leaves, are used to embellish this simple but stunning 30th anniversary design, mounted in a contrasting red circular hoop.

YOU WILL NEED

Navy blue Aida fabric to size,
14 threads/stitches to 2.5cm (1in)
Stranded cotton and Kreinik blending filament
in the colours specified in the key
Assorted trimmings
15cm (6in) DMC circular flexi-hoop

1 Work the cross stitch embroidery centrally on the Aida fabric, using 2 strands of stranded cotton for the cross stitch and 1 strand for the backstitch, and incorporating the Kreinik blending filament as indicated.

2 Mount the embroidery in the flexi-hoop following the instructions given on page 15.

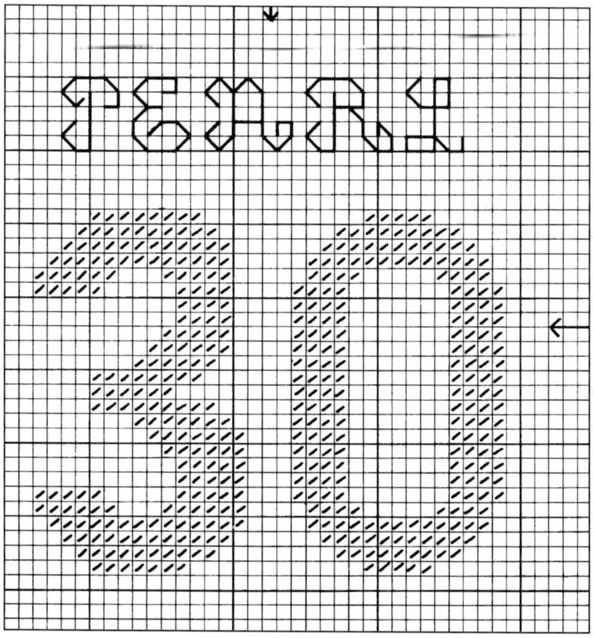

30 YEARS ~ PEARL

◿	White + 032-BF
—	**backstitch**
	White + 032-BF

FLYING HIGH

A pair of bluebirds soar high in the air in this lovely anniversary design.

YOU WILL NEED

White Aida fabric to size,
14 threads/stitches to 2.5cm (1in)
Stranded cottons in the colours specified in the key
15 × 20cm (6 × 8in) Framecraft crafta card

1 Work the cross stitch embroidery centrally on the Aida fabric, using 2 strands of stranded cotton for the cross stitch and 1 strand for the backstitch.
2 Mount the embroidery in the card following the instructions given on page 15.

CELEBRATE WITH FLOWERS

A vase of attractive pink flowers brings best wishes for a wedding anniversary.

YOU WILL NEED

White Aida fabric to size,
14 threads/stitches to 2.5cm (1in)
Stranded cottons in the colours specified in the key
15 × 20cm (6 × 8in) Framecraft crafta card

1 Work the cross stitch embroidery centrally on the Aida fabric, using 2 strands of stranded cotton for the cross stitch and 1 strand for the backstitch.
2 Mount the embroidery in the card following the instructions given on page 15.

FLYING HIGH

ll	**797**	Medium Delft blue
–	**backstitch**	
	799	Royal blue

CELEBRATE WITH FLOWERS

ll	**602**	Medium cranberry
X	**992**	Aquamarine
/	**783**	Christmas gold
–	**backstitch**	
	602	Medium cranberry

BIRTH OF A BABY

LITTLE BOY BLUE

This teddy bear picture in a co-ordinating frame celebrates the birth of a baby boy. It would make an ideal picture for the nursery.

YOU WILL NEED

26.5 × 29.5cm (10½ × 11½in) white Aida fabric, 14 threads/stitches to 2.5cm (1in)
21.5 × 24 cm (8½ × 9½in) mounting board
Masking tape
Picture frame of your choice
or
Materials as listed on page 17

For both:
Stranded cottons in the colours specified in the key

1 Work the cross stitch embroidery on the Aida fabric, using 2 strands of stranded cotton for the cross stitch and 1 strand for the backstitch throughout. Position the design centrally on the fabric for the picture, and following the instructions on page 17 for the gift bag.

2 Mount the embroidery on the mounting board following the instructions given on page 14. Your picture is now ready for framing. Alternatively, make it up into a gift bag following the instructions given on page 17.

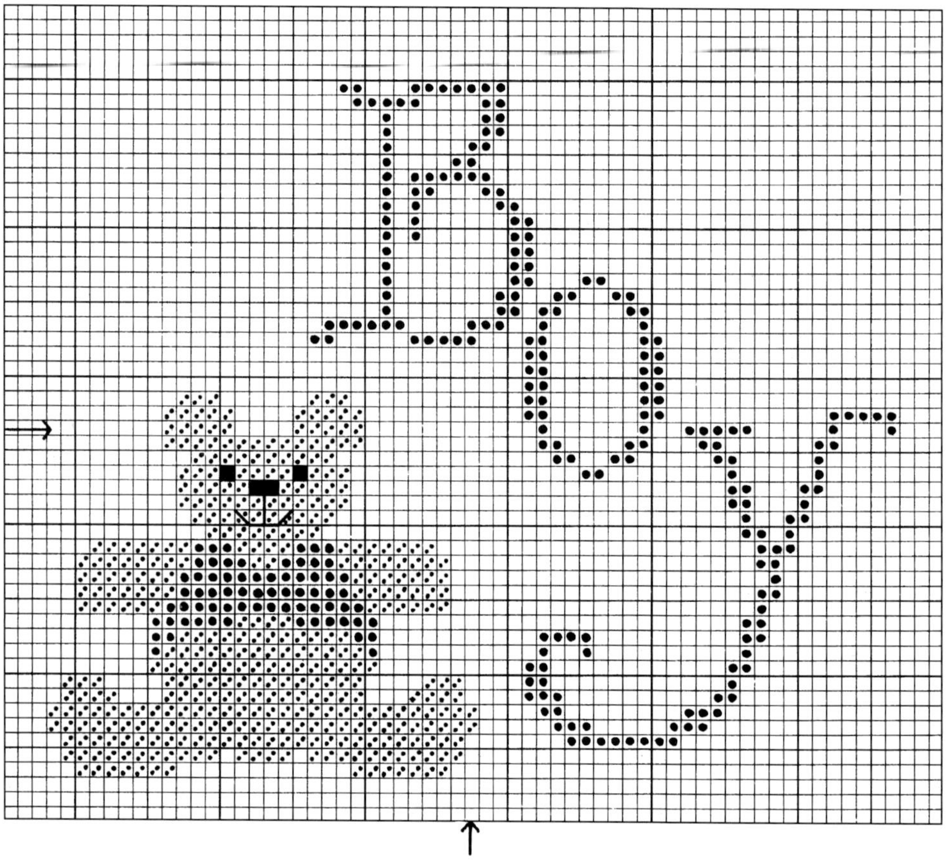

LITTLE BOY BLUE

⊡ (dot in square)	**798**	Dark Delft blue
■	**310**	Black
⊡ (small dot)	**783**	Christmas gold
—		**backstitch**
		310 Black

Boy

NAPPY DAYS

⊞	**605**	Very light cranberry
⊠	**601**	Dark cranberry
☒	**318**	Light steel grey

NAPPY DAYS

Keep baby's nappy pins safe in the special pincushion opposite, stitched in pink for a girl or blue for a boy.

YOU WILL NEED

14.5cm (5¾in) square white Aida fabric, 14 threads/stitches to 2.5cm (1in)
Matching sewing thread
14.5cm (5¾in) square contrasting fabric, for backing
55cm (21⅝in) cord, 4mm (⅛in) wide
Stranded cottons in the colours specified in the key
Small quantity of wadding

1 Work the cross stitch embroidery centrally on the Aida fabric, using 2 strands of stranded cotton. Press the completed embroidery if required.
2 With right sides facing, pin and tack the fabric squares together. Machine or hand stitch around the edge with a 6mm (¼in) seam allowance, leaving an opening in one side of approximately 4cm (1½in) for turning.
3 Remove the tacking and turn right side out. Press again if required.
4 Fill the pincushion evenly with wadding. Turn in the seam allowance, and hand stitch the opening closed.
5 Attach the cord around the edge of the pincushion using small slip stitches.

TWIN TURTLES

These twin turtles play together on the lid of a trinket bowl, or on a card, making a delightful gift to celebrate the birth of twins.

YOU WILL NEED

White Hardanger fabric to size, 22 threads/stitches to 2.5cm (1in)
7cm (2⅞in) Framecraft porcelain trinket bowl
or
White Hardanger fabric to size, 22 threads/stitches to 2.5cm (1in)

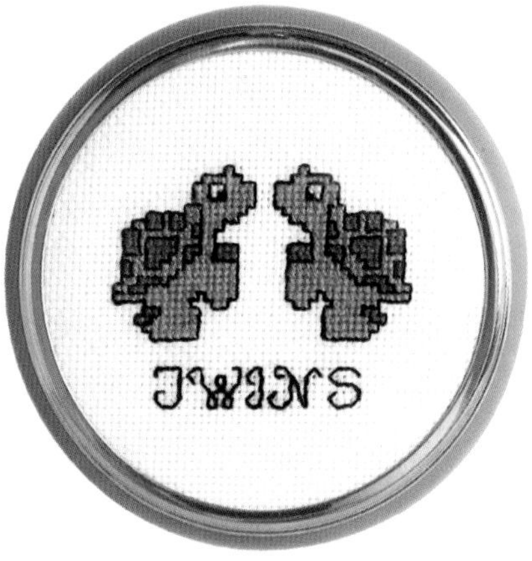

9 × 11.5cm (3½ × 4½in) DMC presentation card

For both:
Stranded cottons in the colours specified in the key

1 Work the cross stitch embroidery centrally on the Hardanger fabric, using 1 strand of stranded cotton throughout.
2 Mount the embroidery in the card or trinket bowl following the instructions given on pages 15–16.

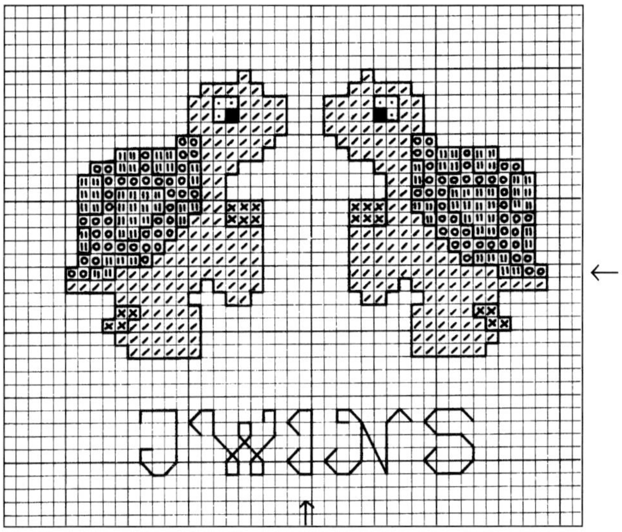

TWIN TURTLES

■	310	Black
⊡		White
◪	912	Light emerald green
☒	909	Very dark emerald green
⊞	632	Chocolate brown
◙	407	Medium cocoa brown
–		**backstitch**
		310 Black

TEDDY TWINS

Congratulate the proud parents of twins with this jolly teddy bear design, mounted in a presentation card or miniature brass frame.

YOU WILL NEED

White Aida fabric to size,
18 threads/stitches to 2.5cm (1in)
9 × 11.5cm (3½ × 4½in) DMC presentation card
or
White Aida fabric to size,
18 threads/stitches to 2.5cm (1in)
7.5 × 10cm (3 × 3⅞in) Framecraft oval brass frame

For both:
Stranded cottons in the colours specified in the key

1 Work the cross stitch embroidery centrally on the Aida fabric, using 2 strands of stranded cotton for the cross stitch and 1 strand for the backstitch.
2 Mount the embroidery in the card or frame following the instructions given on pages 15 and 17.

TEDDY TWINS

■	**310**	Black
◪	**783**	Christmas gold
☒	**301**	Medium mahogany brown
‖	**798**	Dark Delft blue
V	**666**	Bright Christmas red
Z	**444**	Dark lemon yellow
C	**910**	Dark emerald green
—		**backstitch**
		310 Black

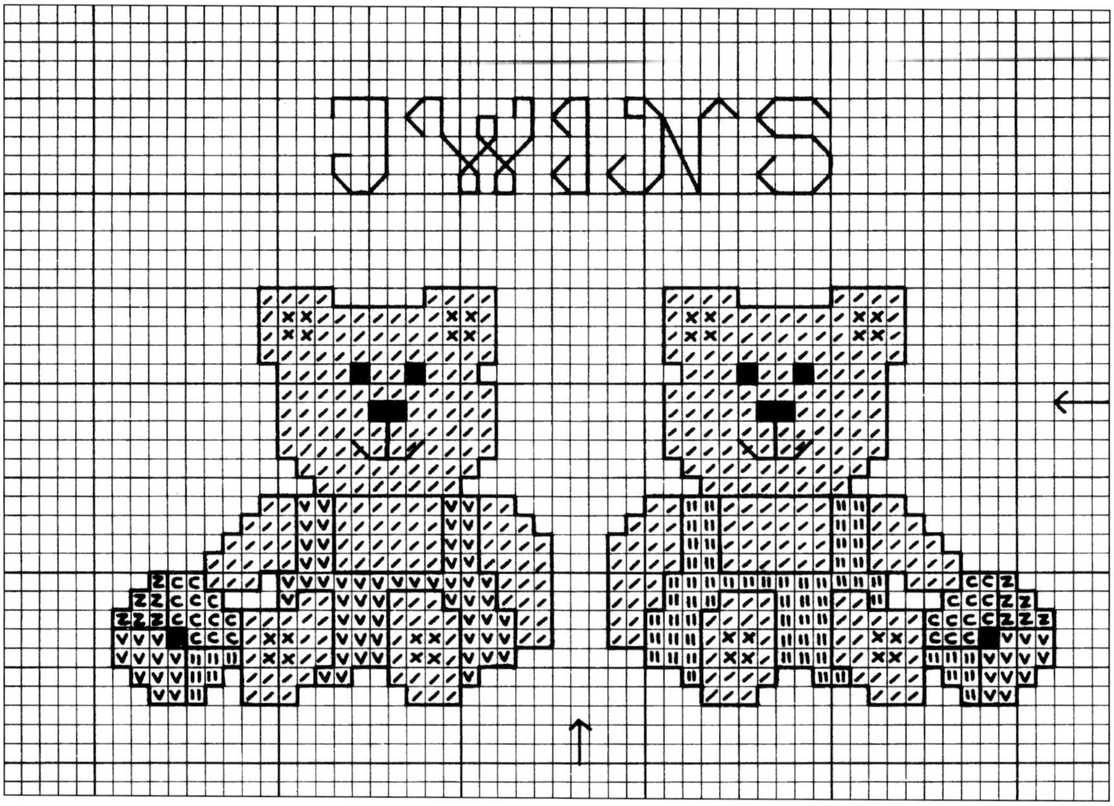

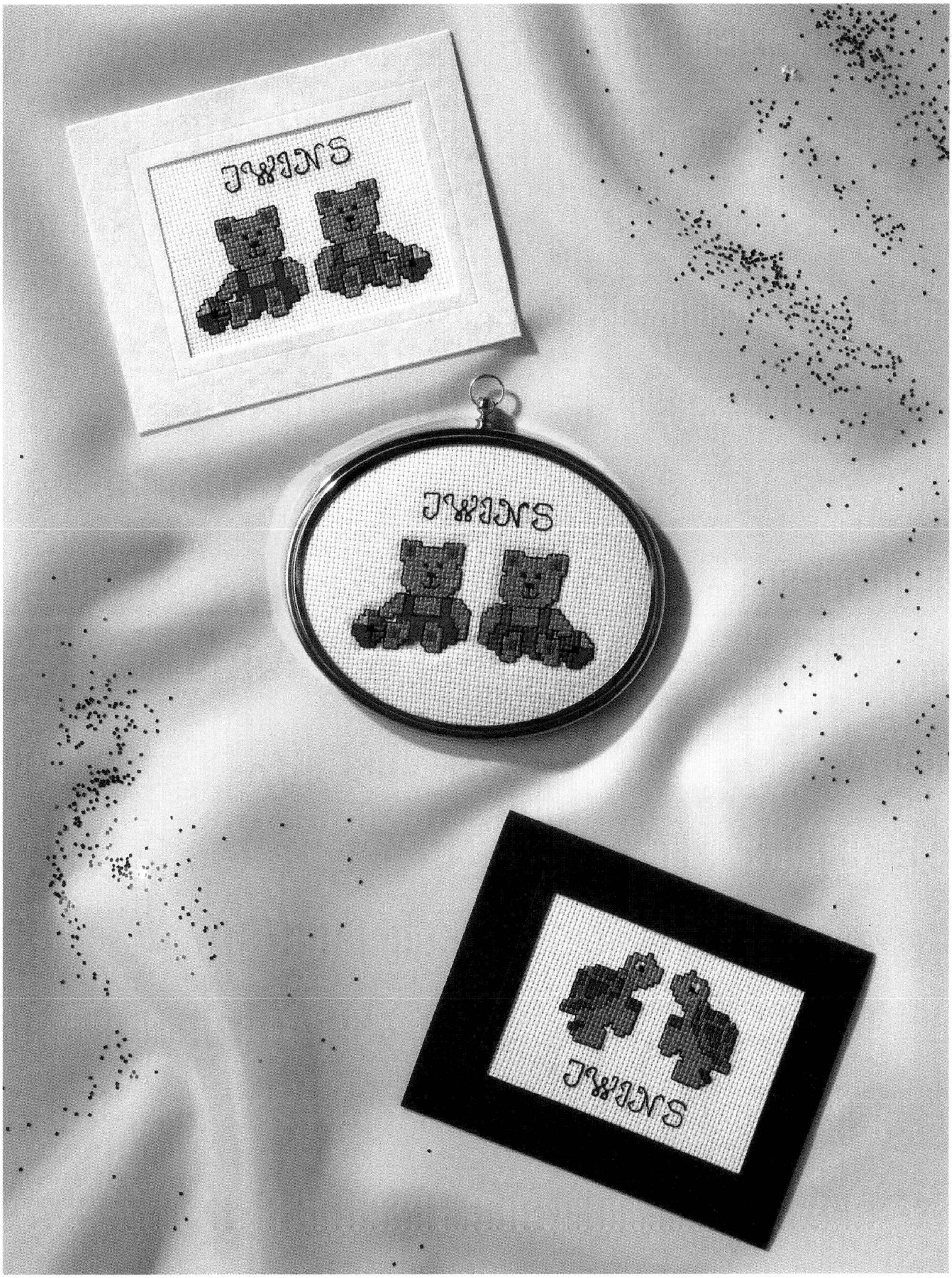
TWINS
TWINS
TWINS

BABY GIRL IS HERE

Stitch a pretty keepsake card in pastel shades to celebrate the birth of a baby girl. Personalize the design using letters and numerals from the charts on pages 124–25.

YOU WILL NEED

White Aida fabric to size,
14 threads/stitches to 2.5cm (1in)
Stranded cottons in the colours specified in the key
18 × 12cm (7¼ × 4¾in) DMC keepsake card

1 Work the cross stitch embroidery centrally on the Aida fabric, using 2 strands of stranded cotton for the cross stitch and 1 strand for the backstitch.
2 Mount the embroidery in the card following the instructions given on page 15.

WELCOME, BABY BOY

Mounted in a special keepsake card and worked in a deep shade of Delft blue, this design welcomes a newborn baby boy into the world.

YOU WILL NEED

White Aida fabric to size,
14 threads/stitches to 2.5cm (1in)
Stranded cottons in the colours specified in the key
18 × 12cm (7¼ × 4¾in) DMC keepsake card

1 Work the cross stitch embroidery centrally on the Aida fabric, using 2 strands of stranded cotton for the cross stitch and 1 strand for the backstitch.
2 Mount the embroidery in the card following the instructions given on page 15.

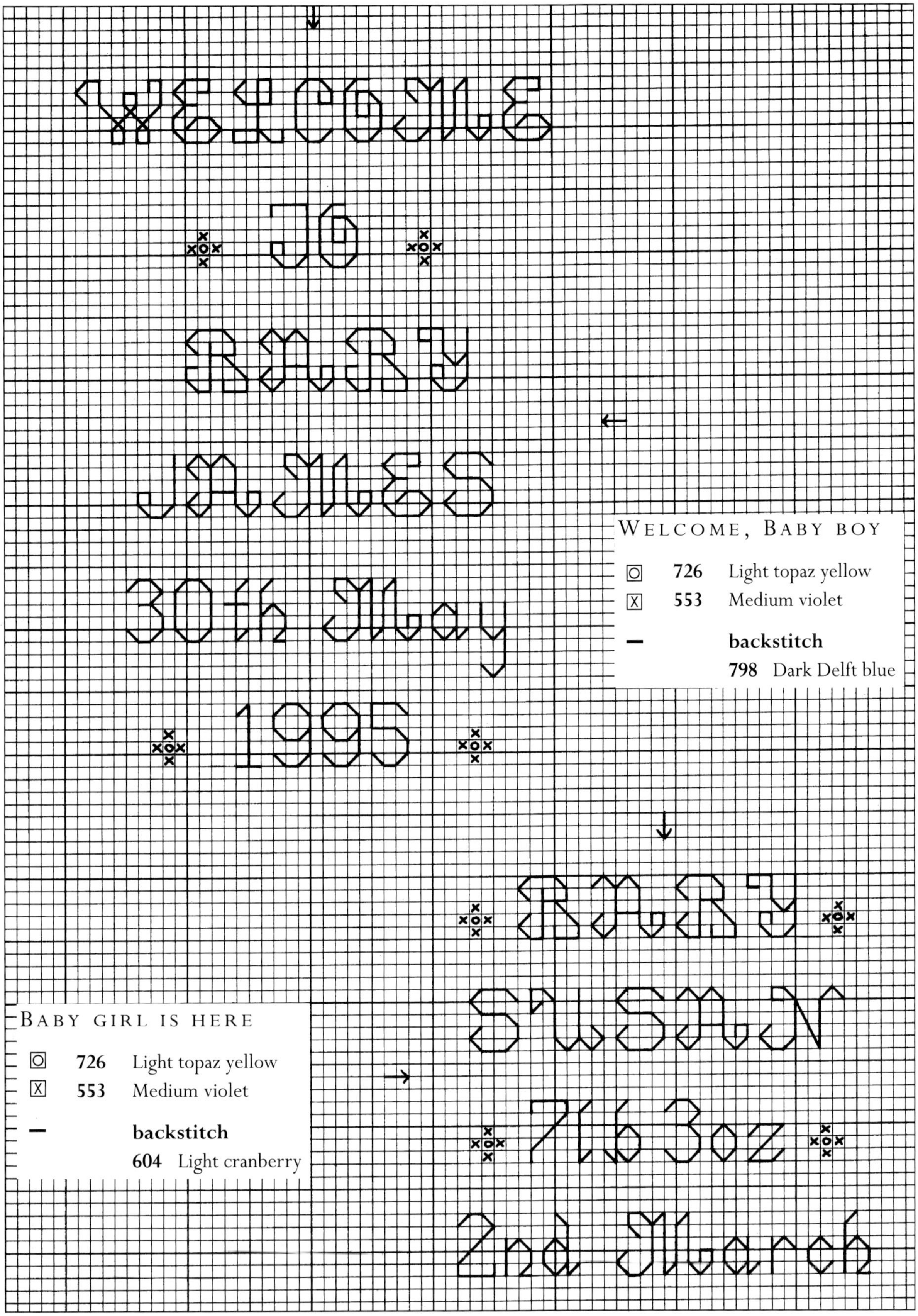

WELCOME, BABY BOY

◙	**726**	Light topaz yellow
☒	**553**	Medium violet
—		**backstitch**
		798 Dark Delft blue

BABY GIRL IS HERE

◙	**726**	Light topaz yellow
☒	**553**	Medium violet
—		**backstitch**
		604 Light cranberry

CHRISTENING

DOVE AND FLOWERS

This delicate dove and flowers design is mounted in a pretty keepsake card or silver-plated trinket bowl to make a beautiful christening gift.

YOU WILL NEED

White Aida fabric to size,
14 threads/stitches to 2.5cm (1in)
18 × 12cm (7¼ × 4¾in) DMC presentation card
or
White Aida fabric to size,
18 threads/ stitches to 2.5cm (1in)
9 cm (3½in) Framecraft silver-plated trinket bowl

For both:
Stranded cottons in the colours specified in the key

1 Work the cross stitch embroidery centrally on the Aida fabric, using 2 strands of stranded cotton for the cross stitch and 1 strand for the backstitch.
2 Mount the embroidery in the card or trinket bowl following the instructions given on pages 15–16.

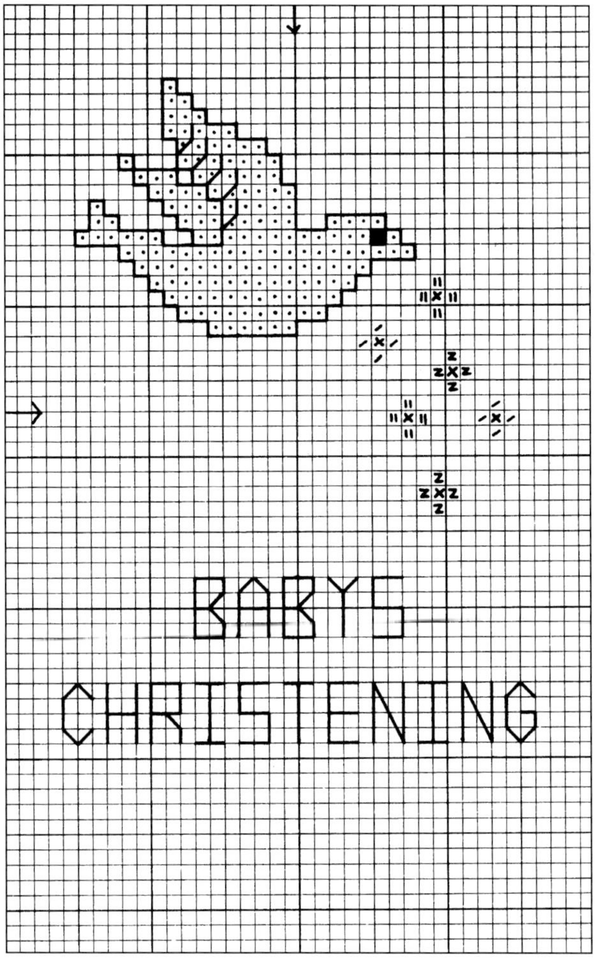

DOVE AND FLOWERS

■	**310**	Black
⊡		White
☒	**727**	Very light topaz yellow
⧄	**553**	Medium violet
‖	**957**	Pale geranium pink
Z	**799**	Medium Delft blue

— **backstitch**
dove **415** Pale grey
lettering **553** Medium violet

SARAH
23rd May
BABYS
CHRISTENING
Congratulations.
BABYS
CHRISTENING

TEDDY BEAR WITH HEARTS

Silver hearts and a teddy bear celebrate a baby's christening, mounted in a keepsake card with an attractive rocking horse design.

YOU WILL NEED

White Aida fabric to size,
14 threads/stitches to 2.5cm (1in)
Stranded cottons and metallic thread in the colours specified in the key
18 × 12cm (7¼ × 4¾in) DMC keepsake card

1 Work the cross stitch embroidery centrally on the Aida fabric, using 2 strands of stranded cotton for the cross stitch and 1 strand for the backstitch, and the metallic thread straight from the reel.
2 Mount the embroidery in the card following the instructions given on page 15.

TEDDY BEAR WITH HEARTS

■	310	Black
▨	783	Christmas gold
☒		Fil argent clair silver thread
—		**backstitch**
	799	Medium Delft blue

PRETTY LITTLE BABY FACE

This frame is designed to be given as a christening present. Change the colour scheme to blue for a boy and personalize using letters and numbers from the alphabet and numerals on pages 124–25.

YOU WILL NEED

24 × 22cm (9½ × 8¾in) white Aida fabric,
11 threads/stitches to 2.5cm (1in)
Stranded cottons in the colours specified in the key
19 × 17cm (7½ × 6¾in) mounting board
Scalpel or craft knife
Masking tape
Photograph of your choice
Double-sided adhesive tape
9cm (3½in) pink ribbon, 6mm (¼in) wide, for hanging loop
18cm × 16cm (7 × 6¼in) thin white card, to back the frame

1 Work the cross stitch embroidery centrally on the Aida fabric, using 3 strands of stranded cotton for the cross stitch and 2 strands for the backstitch. Press the completed embroidery if required.
2 Using a scalpel or craft knife, carefully cut out a central window (9.5 x 7cm) (3¾ x 2¾in) from the mounting board. Place the embroidered fabric face down on a firm, flat surface and position the mounting board on top of it, ensuring that it is positioned accurately. Mark the cut-out on the fabric using a soft pencil.
3 Using a pair of sharp scissors, make a small nick in the centre of the fabric, and then cut diagonally from here up to each marked corner. Place the mounting board over the fabric again, and fold the triangles of fabric to the back of the board, securing them with masking tape. Then fold in the outer edges of fabric, mitring the corners and securing them with masking tape.
4 Fix your photograph into position using double-sided adhesive tape. Form the ribbon into a loop and secure it to the back of the frame with masking tape. Finally, back the frame with thin white card, fixing it in place using double-sided adhesive tape.

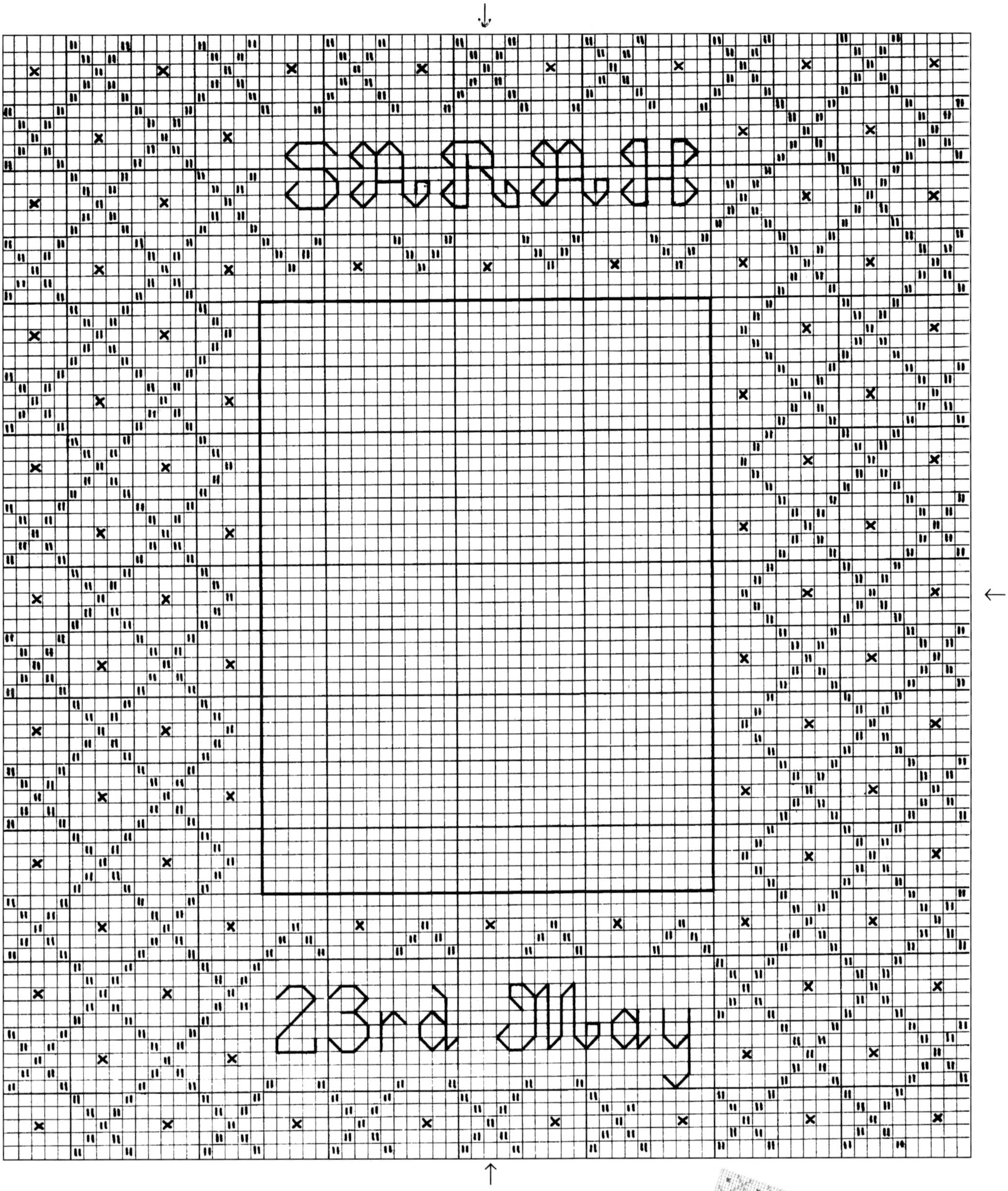

Pretty little baby face

II	**605**	Very light cranberry
X	**603**	Cranberry

– **backstitch**
603 Cranberry

SPECIAL WISHES

AUTUMN WISHES

A beautiful butterfly flutters across an autumnal thank-you card, which is decorated with rosehips and berries.

YOU WILL NEED

White Aida fabric to size,
18 threads/stitches to 2.5cm (1in)
Stranded cottons in the colours specified in the key
10.5 × 17cm (4¼ × 6¾in) DMC keepsake card

1 Work the cross stitch embroidery centrally on the Aida fabric, using 2 strands of stranded cotton for the cross stitch and 1 strand for the backstitch.
2 Mount the embroidery in the card following the instructions given on page 15.

AUTUMN WISHES

■	**310**	Black
⊞ (II)	**433**	Medium brown
⧄ (/)	**946**	Medium burnt orange
☒	**208**	Very dark lavender
⊡ (●)	**435**	Very light brown
–		**backstitch**
		lettering **433** Medium brown
		butterfly **310** Black

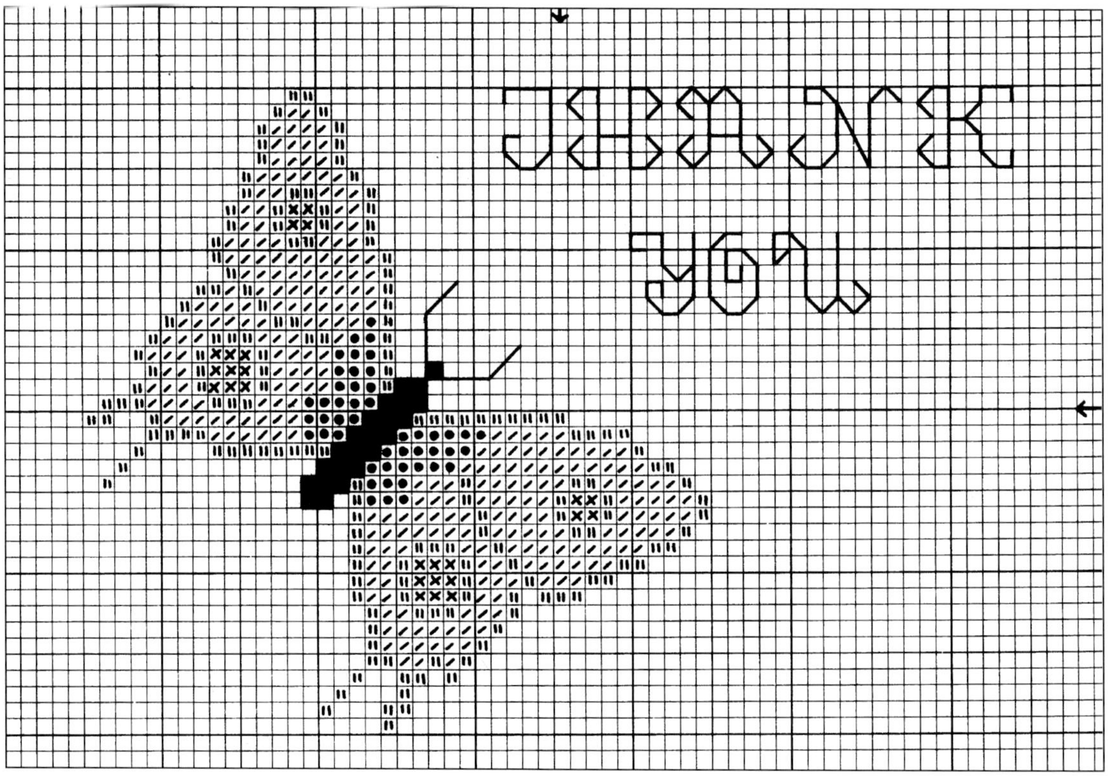

THANK
YOU
THANK
YOU
THANK
YOU

THANK YOU

This lovely thank-you design incorporates the bows featured in the project on page 93 (opposite) called 'Simple Bows'.

YOU WILL NEED

White Aida fabric to size,
18 threads/stitches to 2.5cm (1in)
Stranded cottons in the colours specified in the key
9cm (3½in) Framecraft porcelain trinket bowl

1 Work the cross stitch embroidery centrally on the Aida fabric, using 2 strands of stranded cotton for the cross stitch and 1 strand for the backstitch.

2 Mount the embroidery in the trinket bowl following the instructions given on page 16.

THANK YOU

◪	**913**	Medium Nile green
◫	**553**	Medium violet
☒	**826**	Medium blue
▣	**743**	Dark yellow
–		**backstitch**
		826 Medium blue

KITTY SAYS THANK YOU

This design featuring a grey cat is mounted in a co-ordinating keepsake card, elegantly conveying your thanks to the recipient.

YOU WILL NEED

White Aida fabric to size,
18 threads/stitches to 2.5cm (1in)
Stranded cottons in the colours specified in the key
17 × 10.5cm (6¾ × 4¼in) DMC keepsake card

1 Work the cross stitch embroidery centrally on the Aida fabric, using 2 strands of stranded cotton for the cross stitch and 1 strand for the backstitch.

2 Mount the embroidery in the card following the instructions given on page 15.

KITTY SAYS THANK YOU

◩	318	Light steel grey
◙	413	Very dark steel grey
☒	471	Light avocado green
–		**backstitch**
		413 Very dark steel grey

SIMPLE BOWS

Send your thanks to a friend or relative with this simple bows design, mounted in a domed paperweight to create a practical keepsake gift.

YOU WILL NEED

Lemon yellow Aida fabric to size,
14 threads/stitches to 2.5cm (1in)
Stranded cottons in the colours specified in the key
7.5cm (2⅞in) Framecraft domed paperweight

1 Work the cross stitch embroidery centrally on the Aida fabric, using 2 strands of stranded cotton for the cross stitch and 1 strand for the backstitch.

2 Mount the embroidery in the paperweight following the instructions given on page 16.

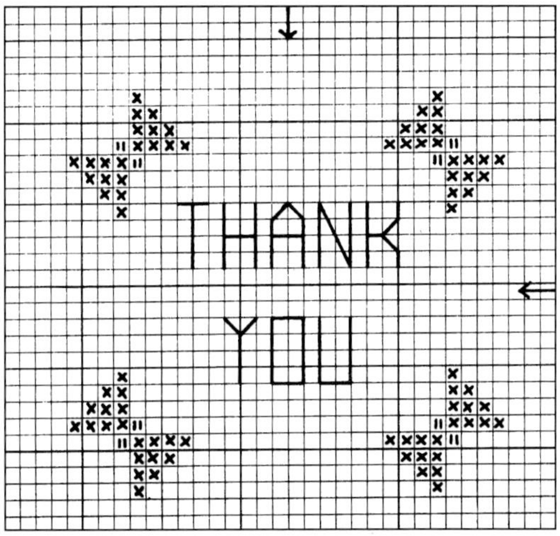

SIMPLE BOWS

◩	913	Medium Nile green
▥	553	Medium violet
☒	826	Medium blue
◙	743	Dark yellow
–		**backstitch**
		826 Medium blue

LUCKY SQUARE

Wish good luck to someone special with this miniature framed picture featuring black cats and horseshoes.

YOU WILL NEED

20.5cm (8in) square white Aida fabric,
18 threads/stitches to 2.5cm (1in)
Stranded cottons in the colours specified in the key
15.5cm (6in) square mounting board
Masking tape
Picture frame of your choice

1 Work the cross stitch embroidery centrally on the Aida fabric, using 2 strands of stranded cotton for the cross stitch and 1 strand for the backstitch.
2 Mount the embroidery on the mounting board following the instructions given on page 14. Your picture is now ready for framing.

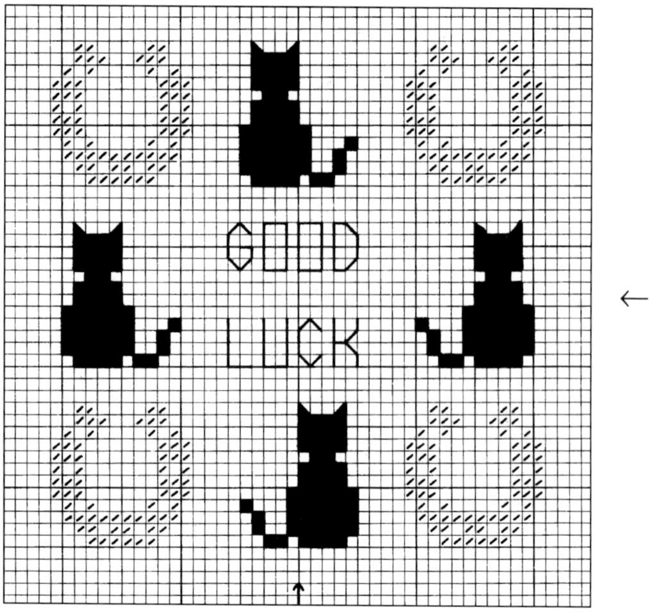

LUCKY SQUARE

◪	**783**	Christmas gold
■	**310**	Black
–		**backstitch**
		310 Black

GOOD LUCK

With the help of a black cat and a golden horseshoe, the recipient of this card could hardly fail to have good luck!

YOU WILL NEED

White Aida fabric to size,
18 threads/stitches to 2.5cm (1in)
Stranded cottons in the colours specified in the key
18 × 12cm (7¼ × 4¾in) DMC keepsake card

1 Work the cross stitch embroidery centrally on the Aida fabric, using 2 strands of stranded cotton for the cross stitch and 1 strand for the backstitch.
2 Mount the embroidery in the card following the instructions given on page 15.

GOOD LUCK

◪	**783**	Christmas gold
■	**310**	Black
–		**backstitch**
		310 Black

GOOD
LUCK
Congratulations
Congratulations
GOOD
LUCK
Well done!
PASSED
WELL DONE

CONGRATULATIONS

Send congratulations on exam success or graduation with this unusual card, which will provide a lasting memento of the achievement.

YOU WILL NEED

White Aida fabric to size,
18 threads/stitches to 2.5cm (1in)
Stranded cottons in the colours specified in the key
8 × 12cm (7¼ × 4¾in) DMC keepsake card

1 Work the cross stitch embroidery centrally on the Aida fabric, using 2 strands of stranded cotton for the cross stitch and 1 strand for the backstitch.
2 Mount the embroidery in the card following the instructions given on page 15.

WELL DONE

Throw away those L plates – this easy-to-stitch keepsake card congratulates a friend or relative on passing their driving test.

YOU WILL NEED

White Aida fabric to size,
18 threads/stitches to 2.5cm (1in)
Stranded cottons in the colours specified in the key
18 × 12cm (7¼ × 4¾in) DMC keepsake card

1 Work the cross stitch embroidery centrally on the Aida fabric, using 2 strands of stranded cotton for the cross stitch and 1 strand for the backstitch.
2 Mount the embroidery in the card following the instructions given on page 15.

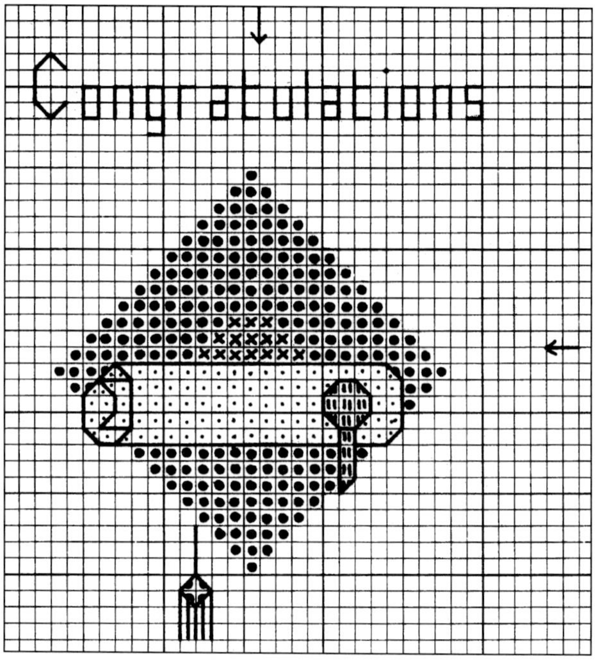

CONGRATULATIONS

●	**310**	Black
X	**414**	Steel grey
•		White
II	**606**	Bright orange-red
—		**backstitch**
		310 Black

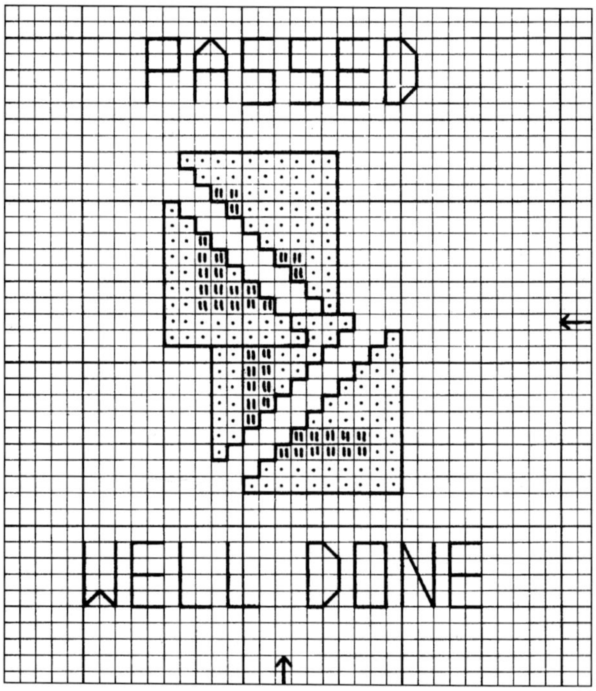

WELL DONE

•		White
II	**606**	Bright orange-red
—		**backstitch**
		413 Very dark steel grey

TIME TO GROW

This pretty design, mounted here in a natural wood frame, makes an ideal retirement present for a gardening enthusiast.

YOU WILL NEED

25.5cm (10in) square white Aida fabric,
14 threads/stitches to 2.5cm (1in)
Stranded cottons in the colours specified in the key
19.5 × 19cm (7¾ × 7½in) mounting board
Masking tape
Picture frame of your choice

1 Work the cross stitch embroidery centrally on the Aida fabric, using 2 strands of stranded cotton for the cross stitch and 1 strand for the backstitch.

2 Mount the embroidery on the mounting board following the instructions given on page 14. Your picture is now ready for framing.

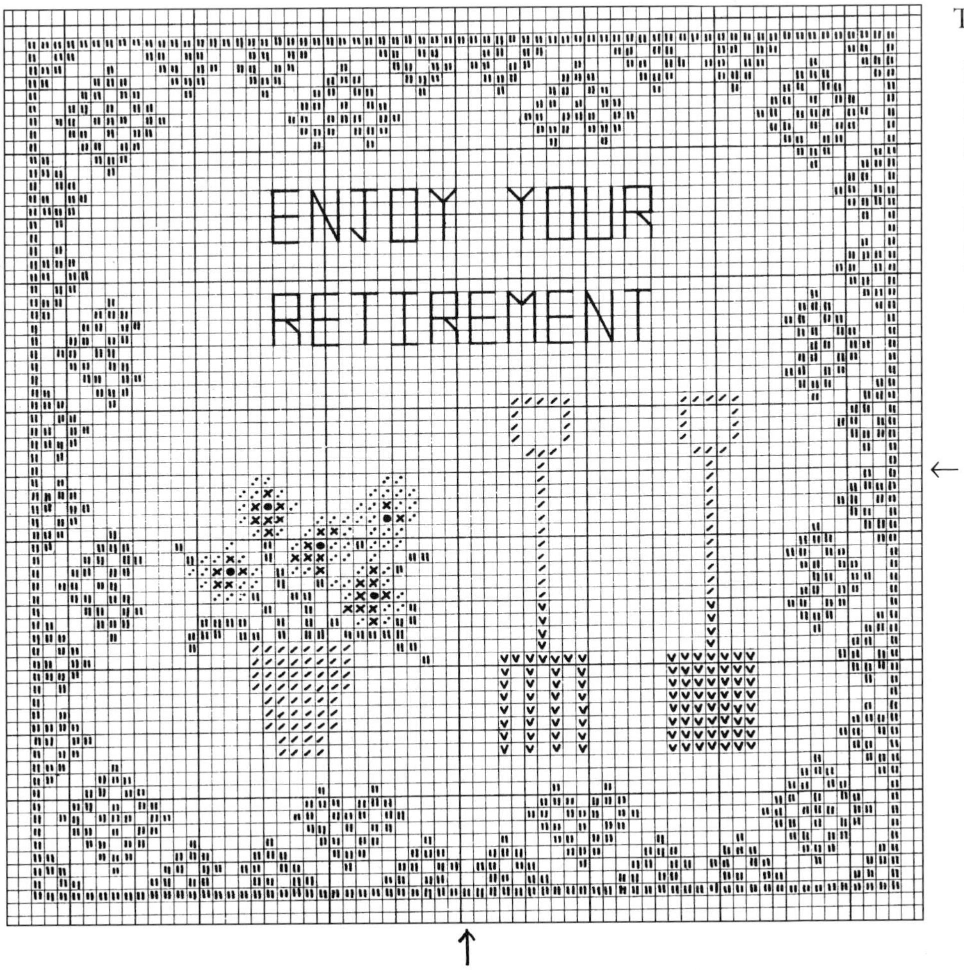

TIME TO GROW

II	**909**	Very dark emerald green
/	**301**	Medium mahogany brown
V	**932**	Light antique blue
•	**798**	Dark Delft blue
·	**722**	Pale orange
X	**666**	Bright Christmas red
—		**backstitch**
		798 Dark Delft blue

ENJOY YOUR
RETIREMENT
ON YOUR
RETIREMENT

THE GOLD WATCH

A traditional gold watch is the theme for this retirement design, which is set off by its toning keepsake card mount.

YOU WILL NEED

White Aida fabric to size,
18 threads/stitches to 2.5cm (1in)
Stranded cottons and metallic thread in the colours specified in the key
20 × 15cm (8 × 6in) DMC keepsake card

1 Work the cross stitch embroidery centrally on the Aida fabric, using 2 strands of stranded cotton for the cross stitch and 1 strand for the backstitch, and the metallic thread straight from the reel.
2 Mount the embroidery in the card following the instructions given on page 15.

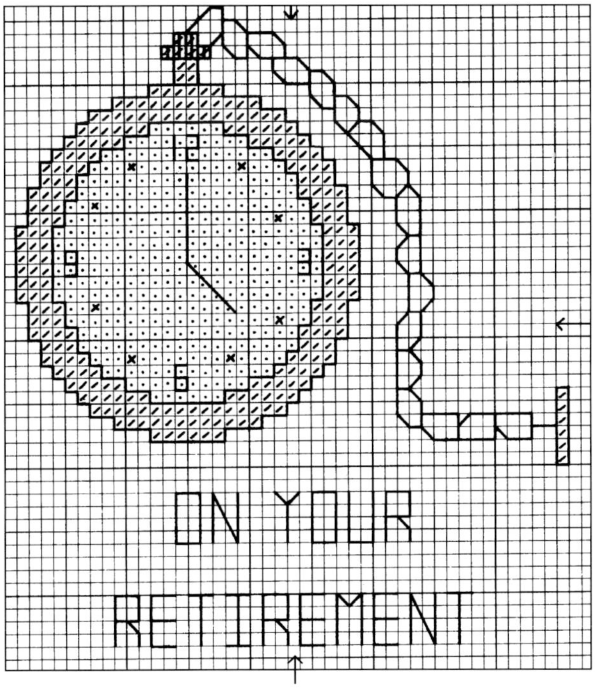

THE GOLD WATCH

⊡		White
◩	783	Christmas gold
☒		Fil argent clair silver thread

— **backstitch**

lettering and nos	**310**	Black
chain	**783**	Christmas gold

DOCTOR TED

This cheerful teddy bear with his first aid bag is sure to cheer up any sick child and enable him or her to 'Get Well Soon'.

YOU WILL NEED

White Aida fabric to size,
14 threads/stitches to 2.5cm (1in)
15 × 20cm (6 × 8in) Framecraft crafta card
or
26.5 × 23cm (10½ × 9in) white Aida fabric,
11 threads/stitches to 2.5cm (1in)
21.5 × 18cm (8½ × 7in) mounting board
Masking tape
Picture frame of your choice

For both:
Stranded cottons in the colours specified in the key

1 Work the cross stitch embroidery centrally on the Aida fabric, using 2 strands of stranded cotton for the cross stitch and 1 strand for the backstitch.
2 Mount the embroidery in the card following the instructions given on page 15. Alternatively, mount

the embroidery on the mounting board following the instructions given on page 14. Your picture is now ready for framing.

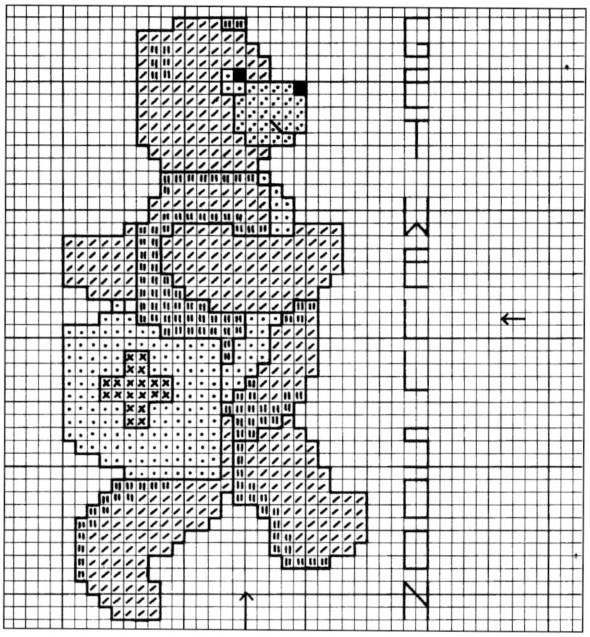

DOCTOR TED

■	310	Black
⊡		White
⧄	783	Christmas gold
Ⅱ	781	Dark topaz brown
⊡	738	Very light tan
⊠	666	Bright Christmas red
V	899	Medium pink
6	975	Dark golden brown
—		**backstitch**
		310 Black

TAKE YOUR MEDICINE

■	310	Black
⊡		White
⧄	783	Christmas gold
Ⅱ	781	Dark topaz brown
⊡	738	Very light tan
⊠	666	Bright Christmas red
V	899	Medium pink
6	975	Dark golden brown
—		**backstitch**
		310 Black

TAKE YOUR MEDICINE

This cute but poorly teddy bear will encourage any sick child to take his or her medicine.

YOU WILL NEED

White Aida fabric to size,
14 threads/stitches to 2.5cm (1in)
15 × 20cm (6 × 8in) Framecraft crafta card
or
23 × 26.5cm (9 × 10½in) white Aida fabric,
11 threads/stitches to 2.5cm (1in)
18 × 21.5cm (7 × 8½in) mounting board
Masking tape
Picture frame of your choice

For both:
Stranded cottons in the colours specified in the key

1 Work the cross stitch embroidery centrally on the Aida fabric, using 2 strands of stranded cotton for the cross stitch and 1 strand for the backstitch.

2 Mount the embroidery in the card following the instructions given on page 15. Alternatively, mount the embroidery on the mounting board following the instructions given on page 14. Your picture is now ready for framing.

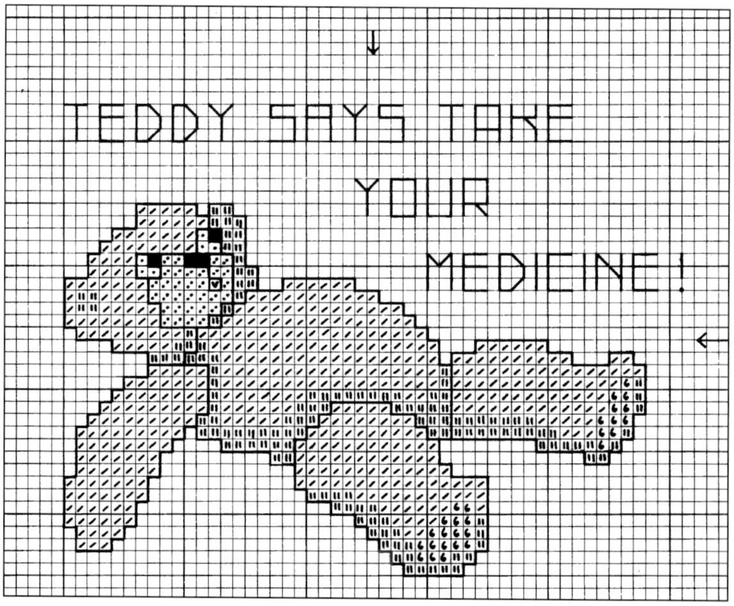

TEDDY SAYS TAKE YOUR MEDICINE!
TEDDY SAYS TAKE YOUR MEDICINE!
GET WELL SOON
GET WELL SOON

GARLAND OF FLOWERS

A 'Get Well Soon' message in this pretty design, mounted in a presentation card or co-ordinating porcelain trinket bowl.

YOU WILL NEED

White Aida fabric to size,
14 threads/stitches to 2.5cm (1in)
15 × 20cm (6 × 8in) Framecraft crafta card
or
White Aida fabric to size,
18 threads/stitches to 2.5cm (1in)
7cm (2⅝in) Framecraft porcelain trinket bowl

For both:
Stranded cottons in the colours specified in the key

1 Work the cross stitch embroidery centrally on the Aida fabric, using 2 strands of stranded cotton for the cross stitch and 1 strand for the backstitch.
2 Mount the embroidery in the card or trinket bowl following the instructions given on pages 15–16.

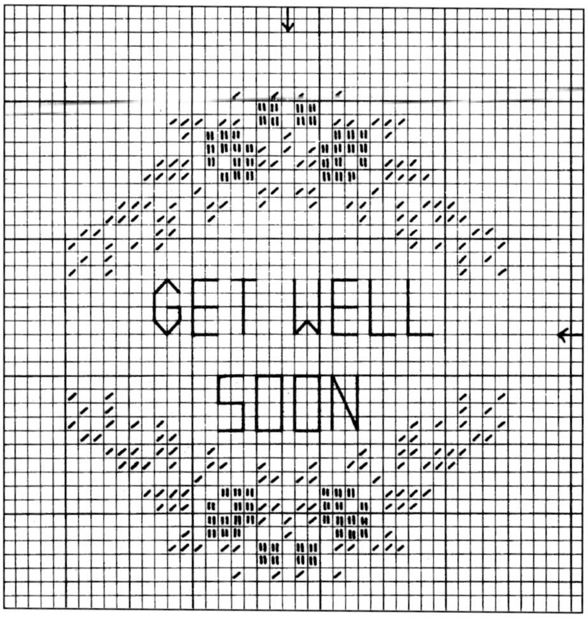

GARLAND OF FLOWERS

⧄	**912**	Light emerald green
II	**956**	Geranium pink
–		**backstitch**
		798 Dark Delft blue

BASKET OF FRUIT

Set a friend or relative on the road to recovery with this health-giving basket of fruit, in warm, cheerful colours, displayed in a smart presentation card.

YOU WILL NEED

White Aida fabric to size,
14 threads/stitches to 2.5cm (1in)
Stranded cottons in the colours specified in the key
15 × 20cm (6 × 8in) Framecraft crafta card

1 Work the cross stitch embroidery centrally on the Aida fabric, using 2 strands of stranded cotton for the cross stitch and 1 strand for the backstitch.
2 Mount the embroidery in the card following the instructions given on page 15.

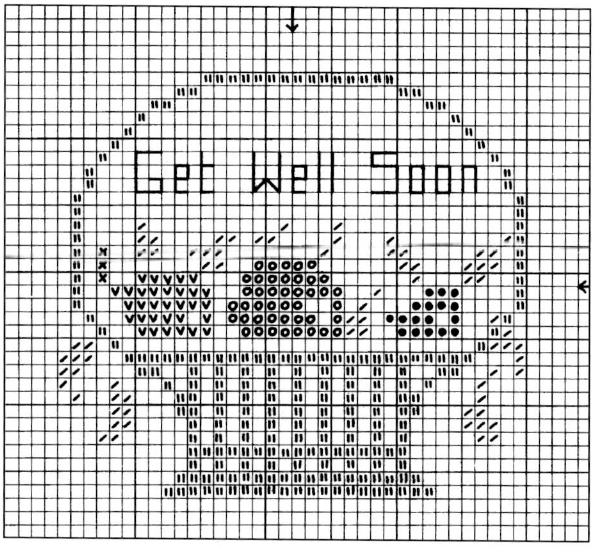

BASKET OF FRUIT

II	**729**	Medium old gold
⧄	**702**	Kelly green
⊠	**435**	Very light brown
V	**3013**	Light khaki green
◎	**970**	Light pumpkin orange
◙	**444**	Dark lemon yellow
–		**backstitch**
		798 Dark Delft blue

Get Well Soon
GET WELL
SOON
GET WELL
SOON

Welcome to your new home

Welcome home

One of these 'Welcome' designs will help the recipient to feel instantly at home in their new abode.

You will need

For all:

Sky blue Aida fabric to size,
14 threads/stitches to 2.5cm (1in)
Stranded cottons in the colours specified in the key

For the house:
12 × 18cm (4¾ × 7¼in) DMC keepsake card

For the apartment and bungalow:
10.5 × 17cm (4¼ × 6¾in) DMC keepsake card

1 Work the cross stitch embroidery centrally on the Aida fabric, using 2 strands of stranded cotton for the cross stitch and 1 strand for the backstich.
2 Mount the embroidery in the card following the instructions given on page 15.

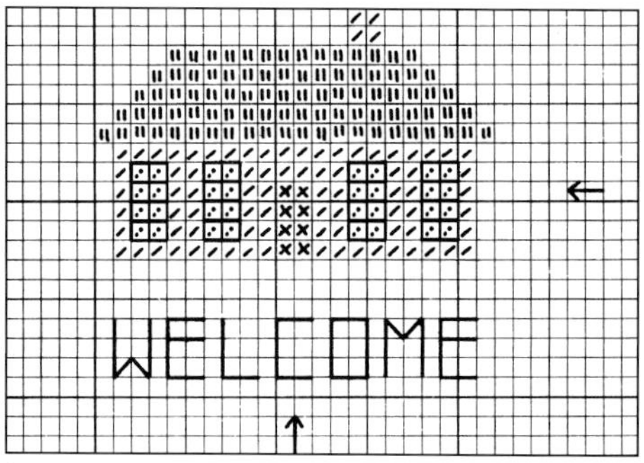

New bungalow

II	**317**	Medium steel grey
⋅	**318**	Light steel grey
/		White
X	**909**	Very dark emerald green
—		**backstitch**
		310 Black

New apartment

X	**927**	Blue-grey
/	**318**	Light steel grey
●	**310**	Black
—		**backstitch**
		310 Black

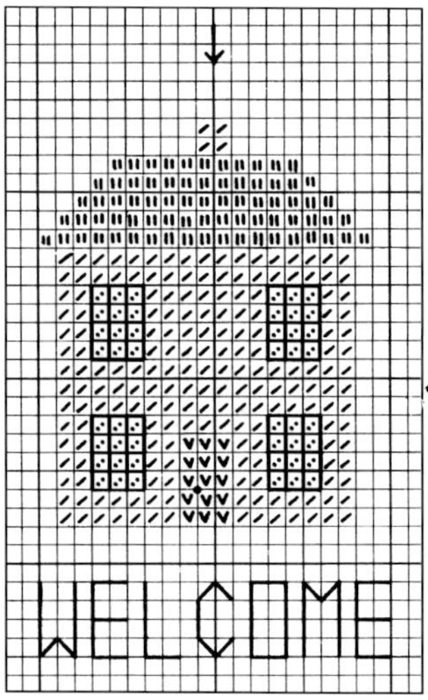

New house

/	**921**	Copper
II	**317**	Medium steel grey
V	**797**	Royal blue + French knot in **783** Christmas gold
⋅	**318**	Light steel grey
—		**backstitch**
	lettering **317**	Medium steel grey
	windows	White

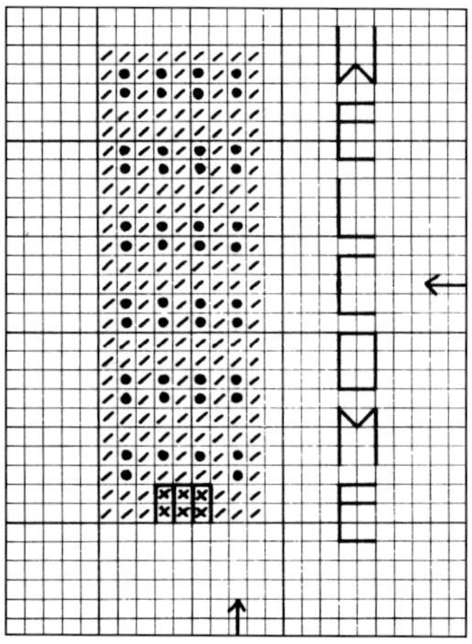

HOME
SWEET
HOME
WELCOME
WELCOME
WELCOME

HOME SWEET HOME

This traditional 'Home Sweet Home' sampler makes an ideal gift for anyone moving into a new home.

YOU WILL NEED

34 × 42cm (13½ × 16½in) white Aida fabric, 14 threads/stitches to 2.5cm (1in)
Stranded cottons in the colours specified in the key
26.5 × 34cm (10½ x 13½in) mounting board
Masking tape
Picture frame of your choice

1 Work the cross stitch embroidery centrally on the Aida fabric, using 2 strands of stranded cotton throughout.

2 Mount the embroidery on the mounting board following the instructions given on page 14. Your picture is now ready for framing.

HOME SWEET HOME

◪	**472**	Very light avocado green
☒	**469**	Avocado green
◫	**3688**	Medium mauve
◙	**931**	Antique blue

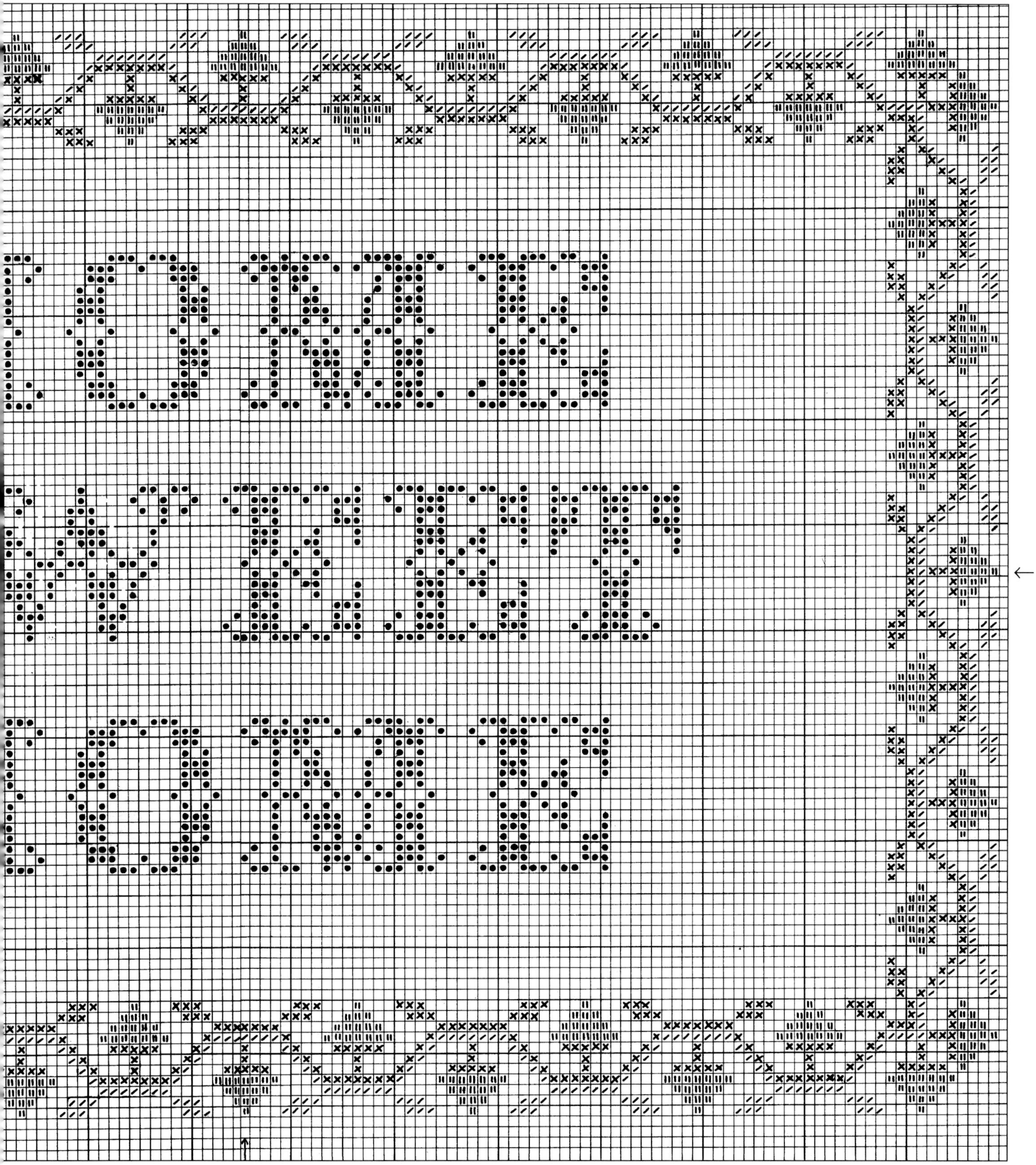

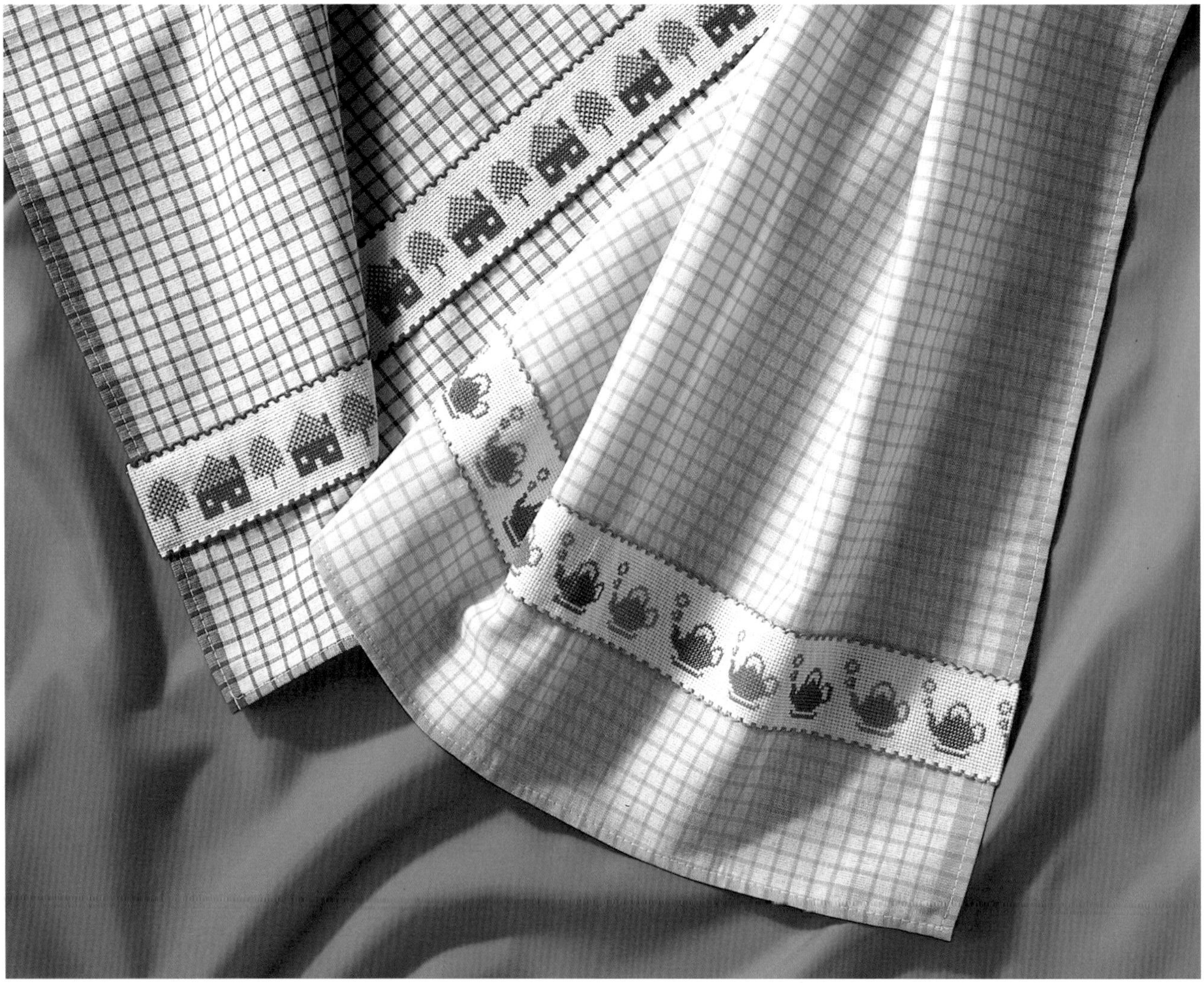

PRETTY REPEATS

The repeat patterns opposite are worked on 5cm (2in) scalloped-edge Aida bands. The bands on the tea towels (above) make a lovely moving present.

YOU WILL NEED

Required length of scalloped-edge Aida band, 5cm (2in) wide, in your chosen colour
Stranded cottons in the colours specified in the key
Sewing thread to match Aida band

1 Measure the width of the tea towel, adding 2.5cm (1in) for turnings, to establish the length of Aida band required.
2 Using 2 strands of stranded cotton for the cross stitch and 1 for the backstitch, stitch enough repeats of the pattern to fill the band, leaving 1.25cm (½in) of unworked fabric at each end.
3 Machine stitch the band on to the tea towel, turning the 1.25 cm (½in) of unworked fabric over to the wrong side of the tea towel at each end.

PRETTY REPEATS

☒	**470**	Medium avocado green
⊡	**349**	Red
Ⓒ	**318**	Light steel grey
⊙	**721**	Orange
V	**420**	Dark hazelnut brown
•		White
—		**backstitch**
		415 Pale grey

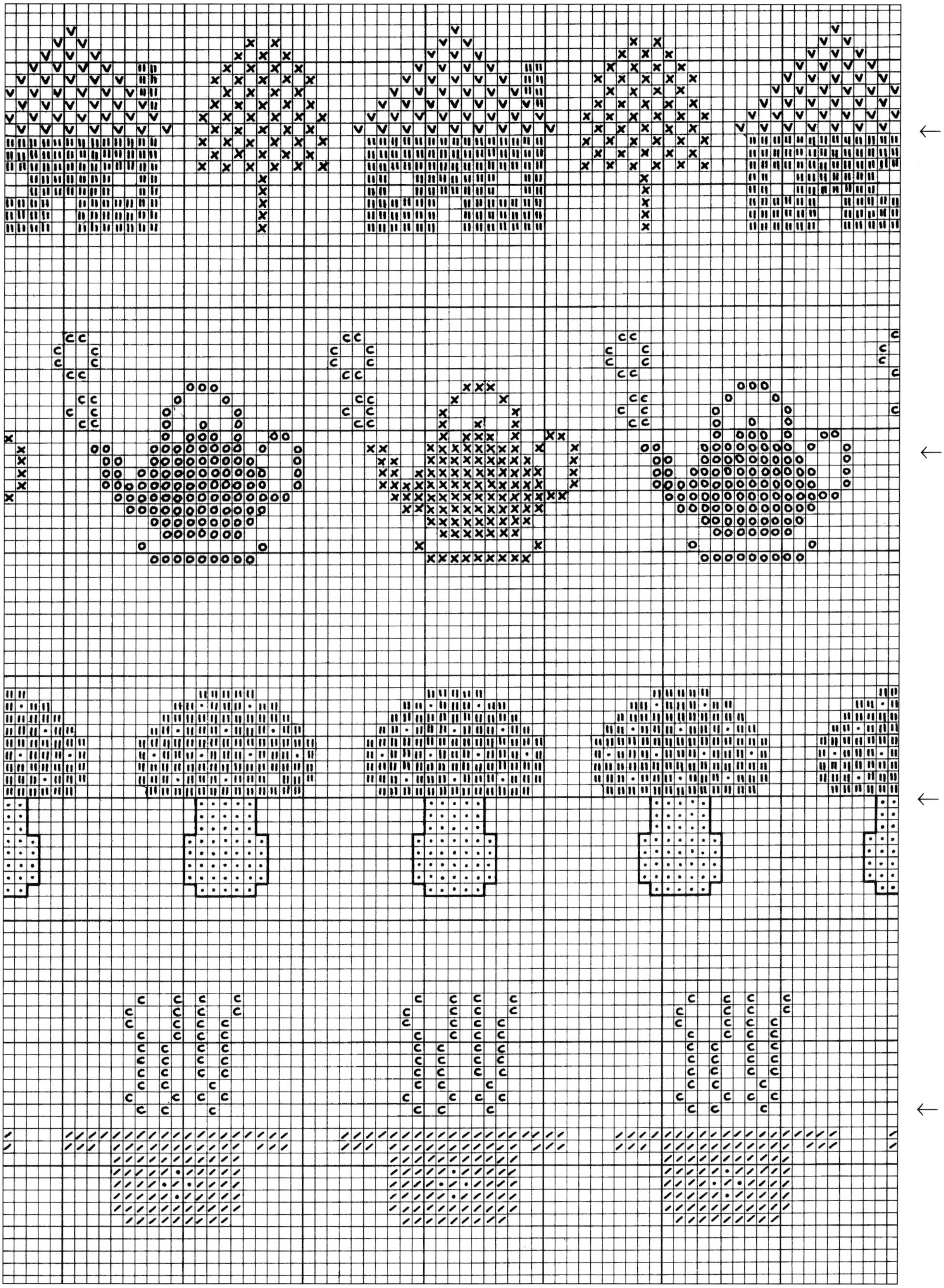

HALLOWEEN

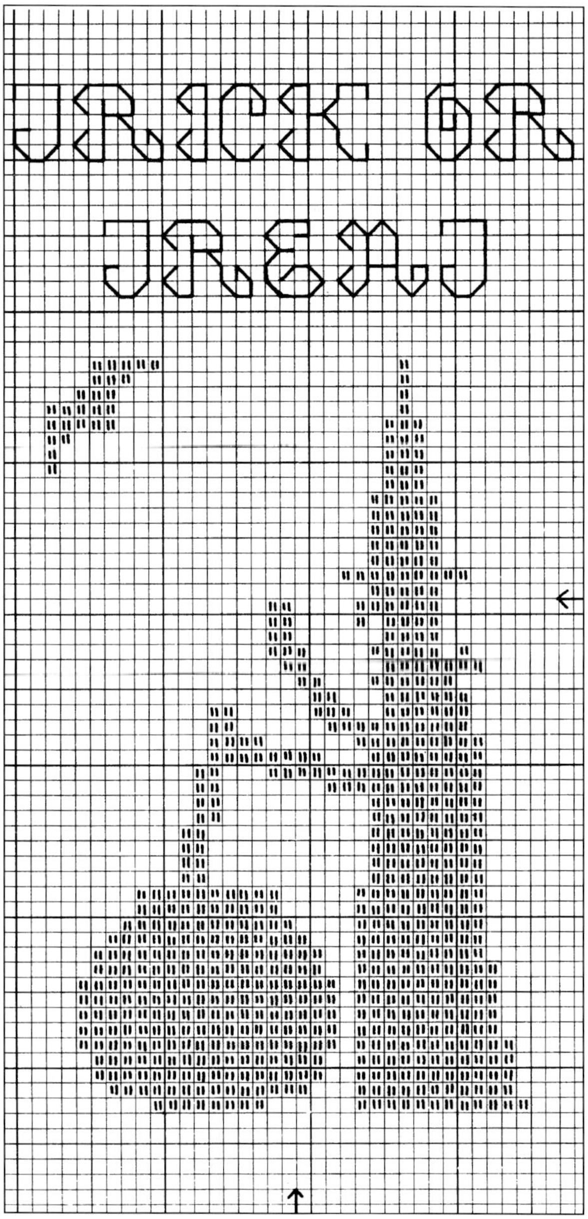

TRICK OR TREAT

⊞	**310**	Black + 034-BF
—		**backstitch**
		310 Black + 034-BF

TRICK OR TREAT

This Trick or Treat bag for Halloween has a drawstring top and is large enough to hold a good number of sweets or small treats.

YOU WILL NEED

23 × 63.5cm (9 × 25in) white Aida fabric,
11 threads/stitches to 2.5cm (1in)
Stranded cottons and Kreinik blending filament in the colours specified in the key
Sewing thread to match fabric
1m (39⅜in) black cord, 3mm (⅛in) wide

1 Work the cross stitch embroidery for the front of the bag using 3 strands of stranded cotton for the cross stitch, and 2 strands for the backstitch, and incorporating the Kreinik blending filament as indicated. Position the design centrally, and 5cm (2in) up from the centre line of the fabric (Fig 1). Press the completed embroidery if required.

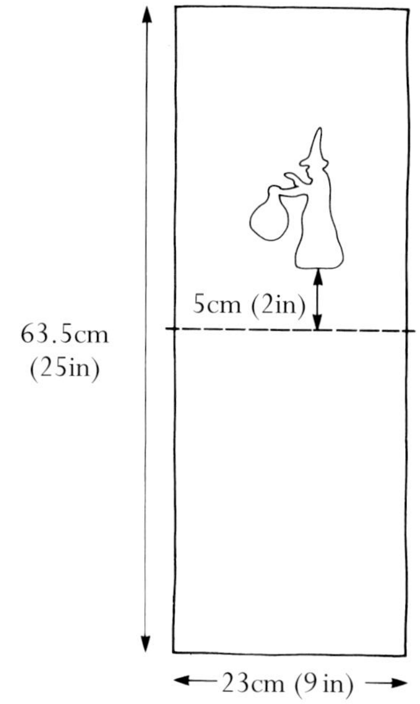

Fig 1

TRICK OR
TREAT

2 With right sides facing, fold the embroidered fabric in half, short sides together. Pin and tack the side seams with a 1.5cm (½in) seam allowance. Stitch the seams by hand or machine, leaving a 2cm (¾in) gap as shown in Fig 2.

3 Cut off excess fabric diagonally across the bottom corners, press the seams open and turn the bag right side out. Top stitch 3mm (⅛in) round the cord openings.

4 On the top edge of the bag, turn over a 5 cm (2 in) hem and stitch in place on the edge of the hem. Stitch again 2cm (¾in) away from this stitch line, to form the channel for the cord. Thread the cord through twice, and stitch the ends together.

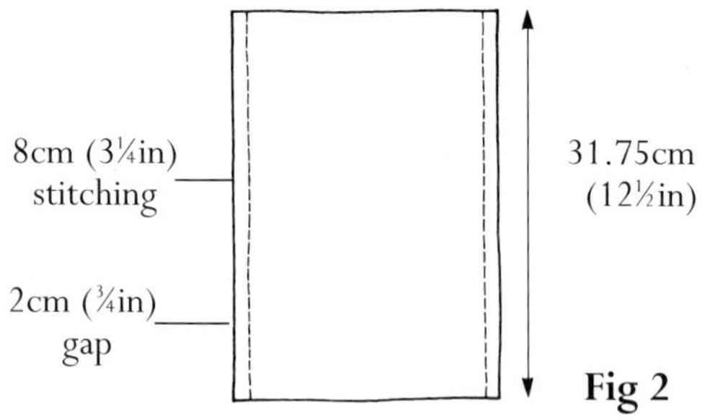

Fig 2

HALLOWEEN MOON

Create a Halloween atmosphere by making this unusual picture, featuring witches' cats and a bat flying past a full moon.

YOU WILL NEED

28 × 33cm (11 × 13in) black Aida fabric,
14 threads/stitches to 2.5cm (1in)
Stranded cottons and Kreinik blending filament
in the colours specified in the key
20.5 × 25.5cm (8 × 10 in) mounting board
Masking tape
Picture frame of your choice

1 Work the cross stitch embroidery centrally on the Aida fabric, using 2 strands of cotton for the cross stitch and incorporating the Kreinik blending filament as indicated, and 1 strand for the backstitch.

2 Mount the embroidery on the mounting board following the instructions given on page 14. Your picture is now ready for framing.

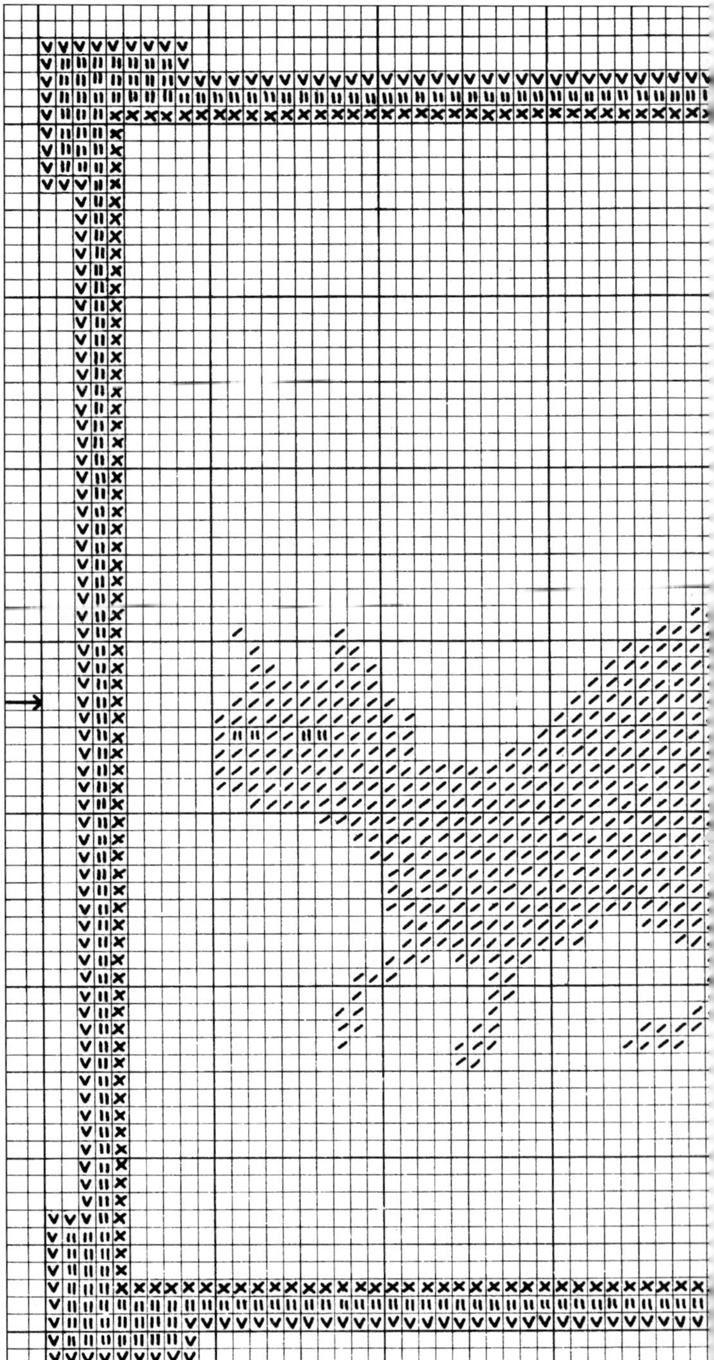

HALLOWEEN MOON

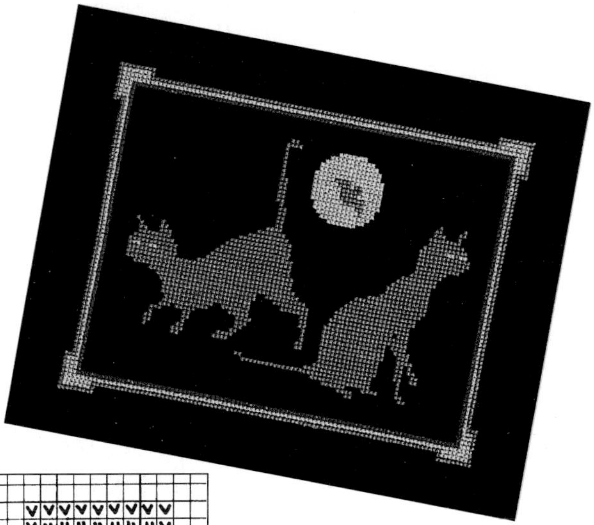

◩	**553**	Medium violet
V	**553**	Medium violet + 012-BF
II	**743**	Dark yellow + 091-BF
X	**917**	Medium mulberry + 024 HL-BF
—		**backstitch**
		553 Medium violet

CHRISTMAS

CHRISTMAS IS COMING

The time and effort involved in creating this advent calendar for a child will be repaid every year, by watching their delight as they discover a tiny gift each day on the approach to Christmas.

YOU WILL NEED

63.5cm × 34cm (25 × 13½in) white Aida fabric,
14 threads/stitches to 2.5cm (1in)
Stranded cottons, Kreinik blending filaments and metallic threads in the colours specified in the key
24 19mm (¾in) brass curtain rings
Sewing thread
55 × 26.5cm (21¾ × 10½ in) white mounting board
Masking tape
24 empty matchboxes
Christmas wrapping paper in colour(s) of your choice
Double-sided adhesive tape
24 brass paper fasteners
4.87m (192in) ribbon, 3mm (⅛ in) wide, in colour(s) of your choice
24 sweets or small gifts
Short length of ribbon or cord, for hanging loop

1 Work the cross stitch embroidery centrally on the Aida fabric, using 2 strands of stranded cotton for the cross stitch and incorporating the Kreinik blending filament as indicated, and 1 strand for the backstitch. Use the metallic threads straight from the reel. Add the name of the child at the top, using the alphabet provided on page 125. Centralize the name in between the bells and holly, filling any empty space with the backstitch hearts.

2 Sew on the brass curtain rings, one for each day, at the position marked on the chart.

3 Mount the embroidery on the mounting board following the instructions given on page 14.

4 For each matchbox, cut your chosen Christmas wrapping paper to size to cover the sleeve section, and fix it around the sleeve using double-sided adhesive tape. Make a small hole centrally in the end of the drawer section of the matchbox, using a narrow scalpel blade or compass point. Pass the prongs of a brass paper fastener through the hole, opening them up on the inside of the drawer. This will provide a knob on the outside of the drawer. Cut your chosen ribbon into 20.5cm (8in) lengths and tie a length around each drawer knob.

5 Fill the finished matchboxes with a mixture of sweets and small gifts and then tie each one to a curtain ring. Attach a cord or ribbon loop centrally at the top of the Advent calendar for hanging.

NICHOLAS
1
2
3
4
5
6
7
8
9
10
11
12
13
14
15
16
17
18
19
20
21
22
23
24

CHRISTMAS IS COMING ~
CHRISTMAS CARDS
AND KEEPSAKES

◫	**666**	Bright Christmas red + 003-BF
∝	**775**	Light baby blue + 014-BF
‖		Fil or clair gold thread
■	**310**	Black
⊡	**666**	Bright Christmas red
V	**725**	Topaz yellow + 028-BF
●	**782**	Medium topaz brown + 021 HL-BF
≡	**910**	Dark emerald green + 015 HL-BF
−	**444**	Dark lemon yellow
O	**783**	Christmas gold
⧄	**910**	Dark emerald green
N		Fil argent clair silver thread
Z		White

∧	**740**	Tangerine orange
F	**518**	Light Wedgwood blue
K	**517**	Medium Wedgwood blue
P	**353**	Peach
⁒	**3608**	Fuchsia purple
T	**917**	Medium mulberry
C	**415**	Pale grey
◪	**816**	Garnet red
L	**3064**	Spice brown
∞	**334**	Medium baby blue
>	**632**	Chocolate brown
Y	**3078**	Very light golden yellow
H	**898**	Very dark coffee brown
X	**317**	Medium steel grey
□	**3364**	Light Loden green

backstitch

310 Black

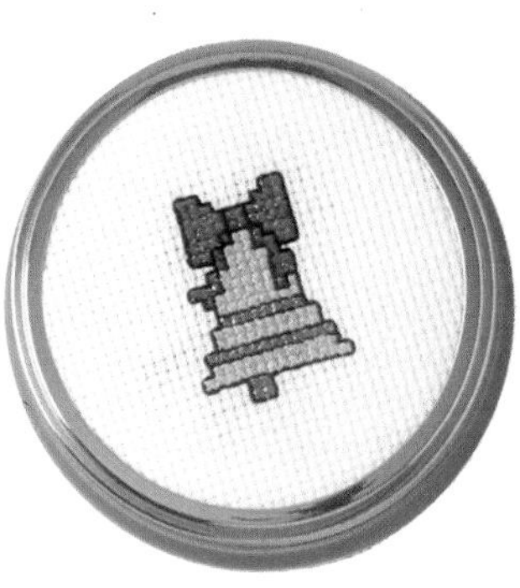

CHRISTMAS CARDS AND KEEPSAKES

Individual motifs from the Advent calendar on pages 116–17 can be mounted in keepsake cards, or used to decorate trinket bowls and gift bags. These would make ideal small presents to hide in Christmas stockings or hang from the tree.

YOU WILL NEED

White Aida fabric to size,
11 threads/stitches to 2.5cm (1in)
17 × 10.5cm ($6\frac{3}{4}$ × $4\frac{1}{4}$in) or
18 × 12cm ($7\frac{1}{4}$ × $4\frac{3}{4}$in) DMC keepsake card

or

White Aida fabric to size,
11 threads/stitches to 2.5cm (1in)
9cm ($3\frac{1}{2}$in) Framecraft enamel trinket bowl

or

Materials as listed on page 17

For all:

Stranded cottons, Kreinik blending filaments and metallic threads as specified in the key

1 Work the cross stitch embroidery on the Aida fabric, using 2 strands of stranded cotton for the cross stitch and incorporating the Kreinik blending filament as indicated, and 1 strand for the backstitch. Use the metallic threads straight from the reel. Position the design centrally on the fabric for the card and trinket bowl, and according to the instructions on page 17 for the gift bag.

2 Mount the embroidery in the card or trinket bowl following the instructions given on pages 15–16. Alternatively, make it up into a gift bag following the instructions on page 17.

Happy Christmas
Happy Christmas
Merry Christmas

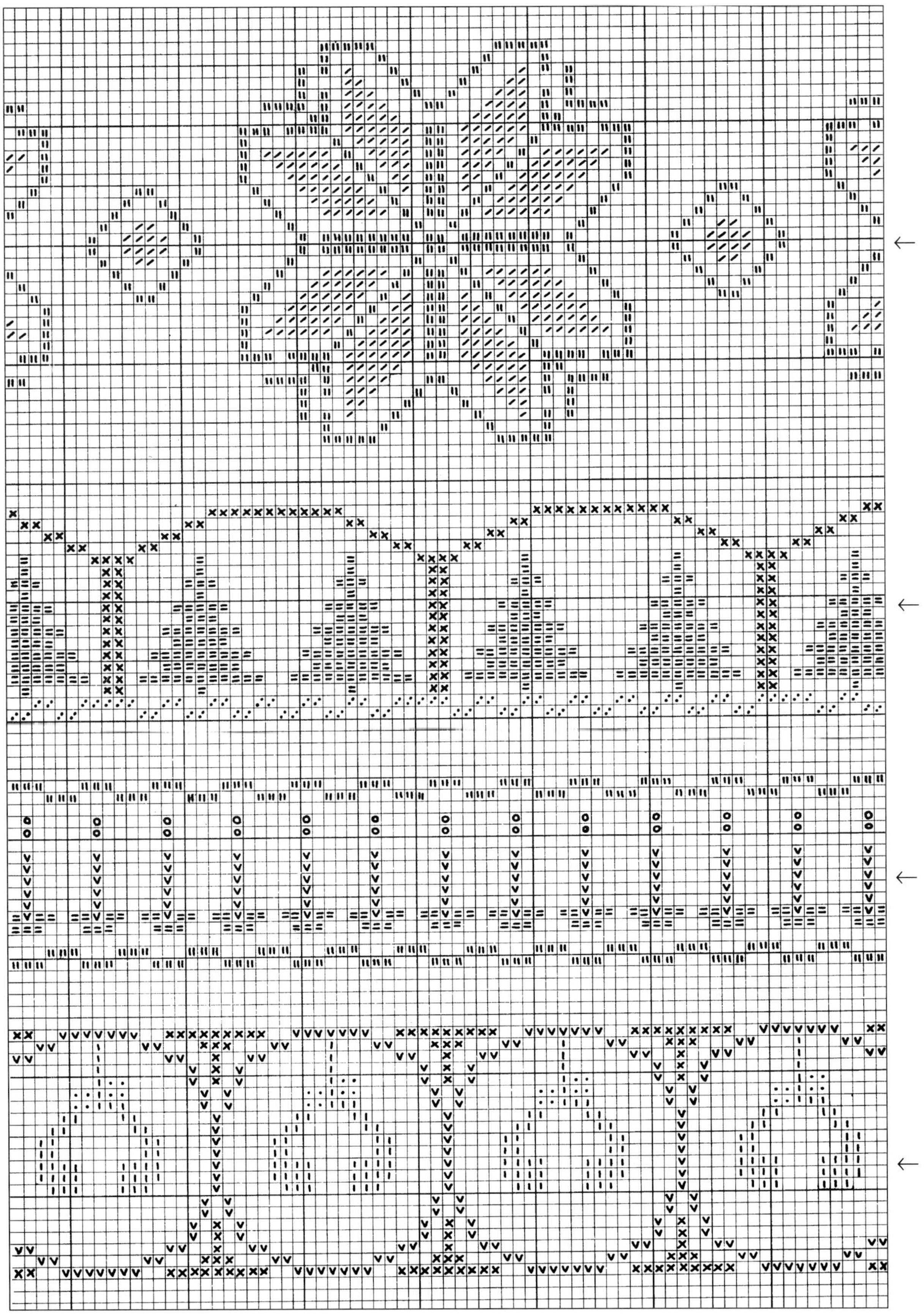

CHRISTMAS DINNER

By adapting the borders from the lower three charts opposite you can create striking placemats.

YOU WILL NEED

For one placemat:

28.5cm × 34cm (11¼ × 13½in) red Aida fabric, 14 threads/stitches to 2.5cm (1in)

Stranded cottons and metallic threads in the colours specified in the key

1 Work the cross stitch embroidery on the Aida fabric in the desired position, using 2 strands of cotton and the metallic threads straight from the reel. Press the completed embroidery if required.

2 To create the frayed edge, remove one fabric thread at a time until you have a fringe 1cm (⅜in) deep all the way round.

CHRISTMAS DINNER

▥		Fil argent clair silver thread
⊟	**911**	Medium emerald green
☒		Fil or clair gold thread
⊡	**415**	Pale grey
V	**606**	Bright orange-red
⊙	**972**	Deep canary yellow
⊡	**3078**	Very light golden yellow
⎕	**3364**	Light Loden green

CHRISTMAS CAKE BAND

▥		Fil argent clair silver thread
⧄		Fil metallise rouge

CHRISTMAS CAKE BAND

Complement your cake with this pretty, reusable band, which fits a cake 84cm (33in) in circumference.

YOU WILL NEED

86.5cm (34in) of green Aida band, 10cm (4in) deep, with silver edging

Metallic threads as specified in the key

Sewing thread to match Aida band

1 Work the cross stitch embroidery centrally along the Aida band, using the metallic threads straight from the reel. Leave 1.5cm (½in) of unworked fabric at each end for the seam allowances; you will be able to fit nine pattern repeats along the band.

2 Press the completed embroidery. Turn under a double 5mm (¼in) hem at each short end. Attach the band to the cake using pins or small blobs of icing.

Gift Tags

Add a special touch to a gift for a special occasion with one of these pretty embroidered gift tags.

You will need

Framecraft gift tag blanks
Scraps of white Hardanger, 22 threads/stitches to 2.5cm (1in), approximately 5cm (2in) square for each gift tag
Stranded cottons and metallic threads as specified in the key
Ultra-soft, medium-weight iron-on bonding web
Soft pencil

You can economize on fabric by cutting a piece large enough for several designs (remembering to space them well), rather than cutting a small piece for each design.

1 Work the cross stitch embroidery centrally on the Hardanger fabric, using 1 strand of stranded cotton throughout and the metallic threads straight from the reel.

2 Press the completed embroidery if required and then iron the bonding web on to the wrong side of the fabric to prevent it from fraying.

3 Place the embroidered design so that it shows through the aperture in the gift tag. When you are satisfied that it is correctly positioned, use a soft pencil to mark cutting lines on the wrong side of the fabric, slightly larger than the aperture. Using a pair of sharp scissors, cut the fabric to size.

4 Place the fabric in position, with the embroidered design showing through the aperture. It helps if you use a small piece of clear adhesive tape to hold part of your design in position before you seal the two halves of the gift tag together. Remove the backing strip from the panel on the left, fold it over and press firmly to seal the two halves together.

You can add a length of embroidery silk or narrow ribbon to complete the gift tag, and write your own message on the back.

Gift tags

N	**783**	Christmas gold
■	**898**	Very dark coffee brown
F	**353**	Peach
V	**436**	Tan brown
●		White
॥	**349**	Red
X	**433**	Medium brown
C	**725**	Topaz yellow
L	**553**	Medium violet
Λ	**911**	Medium emerald green
O	**726**	Light topaz yellow
=	**3326**	Pink
Z	**809**	Delft blue
—		**backstitch**
		310 Black
		Fil or clair gold thread

ALPHABETS AND NUMERALS

A hand-embroidered name, age or greeting provides the perfect finishing touch for special occasion gifts. There are many ways to use the letters and numerals provided here, which have been incorporated in many of the projects in the book. You can even stitch your own personal message using the photographs and alphabets for inspiration.

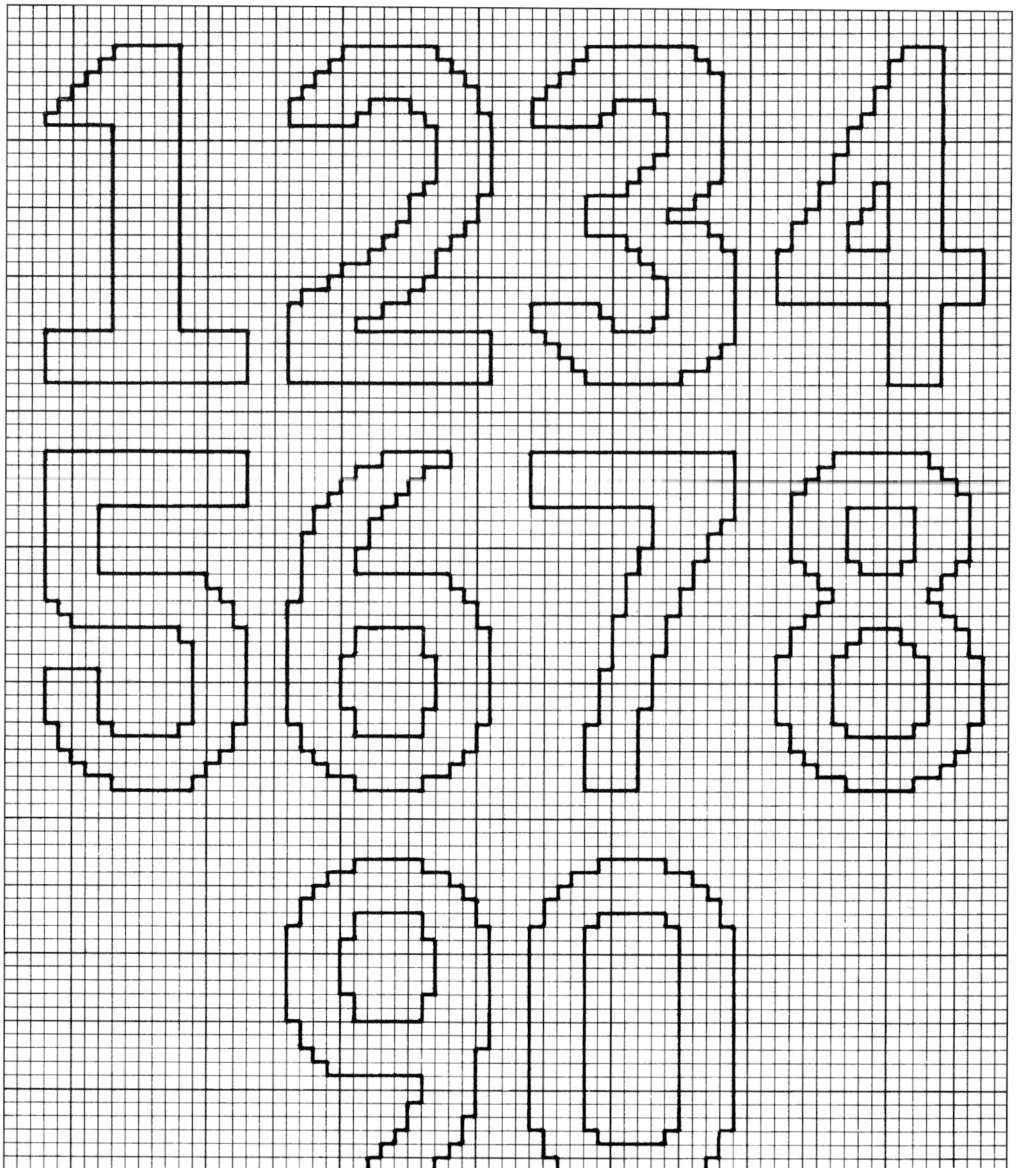

USEFUL ADDRESSES

Framecraft Miniatures Ltd manufacture an extensive range of small frames, miniature boxes, jewellery, craft cards and many other products that can be completed with small cross stitch designs, making exquisite gifts. They are also suppliers of Mill Hill beads. Framecraft items and accessories are available from:

Framecraft Miniatures Ltd
372–376 Summer Lane
Hockley
Birmingham B19 3QA

Ireland Needlecraft Pty Ltd
2–4 Keppel Drive
Hallam
Victoria 3803
Australia

The Embroidery Shop
Greville-Parker
286 Queen Street
Masterton
New Zealand

Gay Bowles Sales Inc
PO Box 1060
Janesville
WI 53547
USA

Anne Brinkley Designs Inc
761 Palmer Avenue
Holmdel
NJ 97733
USA

Stranded embroidery cottons, evenweave fabrics and other DMC products are available from:

DMC Creative World Ltd
Pullman Road
Wigston
Leicester LE8 2DY

The DMC Corporation
Port Kearney Bld
10 South Kearney
NJ 070732–0650
USA

Graph paper for charting designs is available from:

H.W. Peel & Co Ltd
Norwester House
Fairway Drive
Greenford
Middlesex UB6 8PW

DMC Needlecraft Pty
PO Box 317
Earlswood 2206
New South Wales 2204
Australia

Kreinik Mfg Co Inc manufacture a wide range of specialist embroidery threads, including metallic blending filaments. Their products are available from:

Coats Crafts UK
McMullen Road
Darlington
Co Durham
DL1 1YQ

Gay Bowles Sales Inc
PO Box 1060
Janesville
WI 53547
USA

Greville-Parker
286 Queen Street
Masterton
New Zealand

L.C. Kramer
2525 E. Burnside
Portland
OR 97214
USA

Fleur De Paris
5835 Washington Blvd
Culver City
CA 90232
USA

Ireland Needlecraft
Unit 4
2–4 Keppel Drive
Hallam
Victoria 3803
Australia

Serendipity Designs
11301 International Drive
Richmond
VA 23236
USA

Wichelt Imports
RR 1
Hwy 35
Stoddard
WI 54658
USA

INDEX

ACKNOWLEDGEMENTS

I would like to thank the following people for their skilful sewing of the cross stitch embroideries in this book: Diana Hewitt, Lesley Buckerfield, Maureen Hipgrave, Lynda Potter, Jenny Whitlock, Judy Riggans, Andrea Martin, Stella Baddeley, Libby Shaw, Angela Eardley and Odette Coe; and for making up the projects, Connie Woolcott. Thank you all for your lovely work and your loyalty over the years – it is much appreciated.

Many thanks also to Tom Aird for his skilful mounting of the embroideries, and excellent framing service over the last ten years. Also thanks to Janet Dobney and Hazel Nutting, for design ideas. Finally, I would like to thank the following companies who have contributed embroidery threads, fabrics, accessories and graph paper for use in this book: Framecraft Miniatures Ltd, DMC Creative World Ltd, Kreinik Mfg Co Inc, H. W. Peel & Co Ltd.